Permissioned Blockchain
User stories to Engineering

Dev Bhattacharyya

Revised 2.0 for Hyperledger Fabric 1.2 and 1.3
Added Hyperledger Sawtooth 1.0.5 setup
Copyright © 2018 Dev Bhattacharyya

DevbInc

Published by Devb Inc. https://www.devb.com
All rights reserved.
ISBN: 0-9978887-2-5
ISBN-13: 978-0-9978887-2-0

ABOUT

he book, "Permissioned Blockchain" documents blockchain techniques relevant to financial planning and loans origination. The reader is granted a segmented insight into the working methods that help to build run-time processes appropriate to managing blockchain storage, ordinance and distribution. The book represents architectural models, where abstractions of wealth and asset management, and loans and mortgage financial systems meet the concrete.

Permissioned Blockchain comes from several years of experience in modeling the wealth management and lending practice. Few financial models exist in the industry that can capture the services, functions, roles and data relevant to the new networking world of blockchain. The book outlines new methods in transitioning complex applications, encouraging interoperable software development, and defining a set of reusable patterns and modules for the financial services industry by applying the principles of architecture-based development.

Views and opinions expressed in this book are those of the author and do not reflect any policy or position of Hyperledger, Ethereum or any other body or organization mentioned in the book. Examples of analysis performed within this book are examples only, nothing more. The reader must carefully introduce such cases in real-world products as they may have limitations and rely on information of open source products at the time of writing. All attempts have been made to keep the contents abreast with changes happening at Hyperledger.

This book remains a work in progress.

My sincere gratitude to the Hyperledger Composer, Hyperledger Sawtooth, Sawtooth-Seth teams, without them this book could never have started. I am forever grateful to friends and family whose encouragement and patience carried it through to completion.

Paragraphs, design decisions, smart contracts and source code in the chapters are catered with icons to help the reader navigate with ease.

Discussions. Frequently business concepts and explanations.

Smart contract.

Code or implementation.

Alternate architecture. Crossroads.

Certifying and preparing the hardware.

CONTENTS

AWRY BIRDS

The swan sighs "O' the folly of man"
for every chain lost
another block shall live
Man will forever fight man
for all who may live
the life may he give

    Undisclosed pining, the eagle knows not
    no coins can he find
    only ledgers of trust
    spring of hope, he hasn't thought
    When tomorrow arrives
    today's trials will be behind

And, the lapwing flutters
The supper,
her last proof of work,
bitter is the byte
Mouthful, she cries at the dusked western sun
"Did you do it?
 Did you just block the dark!"

Dev Bhattacharyya

FINANCIAL PLANNING
AND BLOCKCHAIN CONCEPTS

 Financial Planning AKA Wealth Management is a broad concept in the financial services industry. Client psychology, which frequently dictates the tone of financial planning comes from historical successes or failures in past investment. Such psychological makeup often drives the contents and quantum of an individual's financial portfolio.

The profession involving financial planning is peppered with Money, Portfolio and Wealth Managers. Wealth Management is not just investment and private banking; it has definitions and boundaries of its own that call for a reference model, limited portions of which can partake in the blockchain technology.

As is evident, 'blockchain-ed network' is not one size that fits all, and this book steers clear of situations that do not warranty its use. Over the last twenty odd years, Wealth Management has evolved into a style of administering that requires good skills in financial planning. As Harold Evensky cites in his book, wealth management is the main discipline of financial planning. Any wealth management machinery therefore must aim to understand the client well – his or her dreams, goals and fears. Newer and stronger robotics and process-automation promises the possibility of advisory algorithms that can tailor for the client, a good, robust portfolio, but that is yet another matter. This book instead, cites a framework on how the blockchain technology manages financial portfolios, advisory interactions, tracks the goals and constraints with ease.

What is Wealth Management?

 There always existed a practice of money management, focused and institutional. The impetus to such comes from a mindset where a person wants to make the most of financial returns.

 In financial terms, Portfolio Management, a comprehensive bulk of wealth management is all about cleverly separating the portfolio of investments through asset class diversification. Inexpensive optimizers, even free ones and prepackaged portfolios represent this form of investment. The portfolio or asset manager stays diverse with multiple asset classes unlike money management which stays focused on a single asset class. Focusing, planning and investing to meet the client's specific needs becomes paramount in the wealth management domain.

When interacting with large and complex manifesto of diverse investments, several activities overlook its planning and execution.

- Gathering related data
- Helping the customer in setting goals
- Identifying financial and non-financial issues
- Preparing alternatives
- Providing recommendation
- Processing the transactions
- Reviewing the plan sporadically

"Permissioned Blockchain" focusses on financial solutions for wealth management and lending using Blockchain and other disruptive technologies to meet the client's discretely customized plan and track the results.

Chapter one introduces the wealth line of business to the aspiring blockchain architect, the experienced advisor and everyone in between. In consulting engagements, it comes as striking that as systems evolve through adoption of coarser and leaner technologies, much of the intrinsic knowledge and expertise in these specialized lines of businesses become lost. The book intends to offer wealth management and lending referenceable models enacted through the new world of networking as pertinent to blockchains only.

This book is about the implications of architecture and technology for the financial industry, namely the new strain called FinTech. It is shrink-wrapped with distinct examples from the financial domain where the need for blockchain runs strong.

It may also include several abstract ideas on where the industry model may emerge. Throughout the book, the approach stays more pragmatic than a mere "top-down" one. Choice of a realistic method lends to the fact, that an insignificant part of Asset Management methods is truly "green-fields", suggesting several processes are not just proven, but run optimally, having gathered much polish over the years. But in the disruptive world of distributed technology, are these processes even relevant? While the answer to that question will emerge as we progress, the pragmatic method provides a clear approach to situations such as mergers and acquisitions or IT Transformations - typical problems that confront the financial industry today.

A coherent description of enterprise architecture provides insight, enables communication among stakeholders and guides complicated change processes. Regrettably, so far, no enterprise architecture description language exists that downright enables integrated enterprise modeling, because for each architectural domain, architects use their own modeling techniques and concepts, tool support and visualization techniques. Concepts in this book outline such integrated language related to architectural domains. In this format, concepts for describing the relationships between architecture descriptions at the business, application, and technology levels play a central role, related to the ubiquitous problem of business–technology alignment, while each architectural domain that is modeled, conforms to standards of UML. Chiefly, usage of services offered by one layer to another plays an important role in relating the behavior aspects of the layers. Structural aspects of these logical layers are allowed to shake hands through a well-defined interface such as REST.

Reverting our attention on how the wealth management institutions operate today - yes, in the heart of the conservative, financial services sector, wealth line of business splits into front, middle and back office.

Though every "office" is unique, they cohesively play an important role in making sure that the bank makes money, the bank has good customer insight and can manage risks. The front office generates the bank's revenue and comprises several divisions like sales and marketing. Middle office supports risk management, financial control, corporate treasury, corporate strategy and compliance. In due course, the goal of middle office is to safeguard the line of business from engaging in activities detrimental to the bank's overall health. Back office includes operations and technology, providing support to the front office to do its jobs needed to make money and satisfy the customer.

Such traditional structure, as you may well discern, reeks of a rigid and bureaucratic governance. It also boasts of a highly centralized and authoritarian operations.

In the new world, such offices become a blur. Users can invoke most operations through clear interactions between software layers making older systems redundant. Distribution of data adds yet another dimension to the evolving ecosystem. Data will soon live through nodal replication and algorithmic consensus.

Blockchain and Distributed Ledger

Power of Blockchain comes from its ability to transfer assets and sustain an immutable history of such transactions. Distributed ledger technology, a critical module of blockchain fits the needs of a person who purports a portfolio of all his or her financial assets. When we add newer assets or revise the older ones, the ledger system maintains and manages the financial portfolio reflecting these changes. It however, can only do minimal client goal checking and constraints management.

Blockchain data can capture every committed transaction as chronological records, besides switching 'on' its ability to run "smart contracts. What gets implied by a smart contract is the ability to embed *business rules* within the blockchain architecture to transact assets[1] between participants. Likewise.

Hyperledger Composer[2] is an application development framework that helps you create applications that use the Hyperledger® Fabric™ blockchain. It contains APIs, a modeling language, and a programming model you define and deploy business networks and applications with, enabling participants to run transactions and exchange assets in such a network. Hyperledger Composer uses the construct of JavaScript programming language to express APIs that make the process of submitting transactions, standardized and easy. It also allows the participating user to create, retrieve, update, and delete assets within asset registries maintained by the system.

---

[1] A real estate, it's title, bank account, mortgage, financial portfolio, coin currency, digital music file are examples of assets
[2] https://hyperledger.github.io/composer/latest/

Blockchain applicable to wealth management

The proposed blockchain financial planning application consists of a consensus managed database of record for a customer, with no elaborate algorithms. A decidedly abstracted view of wealth management process (*as in Figure 1*) breaks down into five different activities. Historically, as in the past, the five processes become the new way of running counsel, disclosures, portfolio management and reviews that can work flawlessly in the underworld of blockchain.

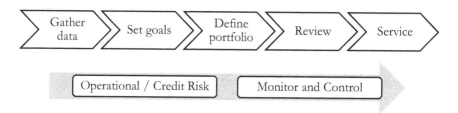

Figure 1 – Applicable wealth management phases

Managing and planning Finances

Extending the process of gathering data, the activities in financial planning extend to knowing the customer, knowing the fears and suspicions, managing expectations and collecting such information unobtrusively.

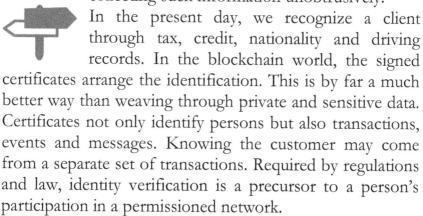 In the present day, we recognize a client through tax, credit, nationality and driving records. In the blockchain world, the signed certificates arrange the identification. This is by far a much better way than weaving through private and sensitive data. Certificates not only identify persons but also transactions, events and messages. Knowing the customer may come from a separate set of transactions. Required by regulations and law, identity verification is a precursor to a person's participation in a permissioned network.

Transactions that occur during verification of a person are often transient and considered 'significant' only for a certain number of days. Therefore, the blockchain application beckons a quick set of activities external to itself.

Once the application admits the person into the blockchain network, every other member of that network begins to trust the person as 'genuine', having the right credentials, and having the right empowerments for controlled access to many artifacts and assets.

The UML class model (*as in Figure 2*) illustrates the nuts and bolts of a client's identification and verification in the traditional way of conducting business, and how it evolves in the '*blockchain-ed*' world. Not just with blockchain, identity in future will no longer have to expose sensitive information. What used to be KYC or *Know Your Customer* changes to the *Revealed Client* in the *Permissioned Blockchain-ed* world.

The question hence goes deeper on how accurate is the person's identity? Does the word '*identity*' have any relevance in the blockchain world, the way we perceive identity today? Is the person and contract trustworthy enough? Or, is there a perceived security threat?

Even a concept like *employment* paraded in the model, simply gets outmoded in the future. *Profession* takes precedence over *employment* where reliability and trust come from how others perceive the client.

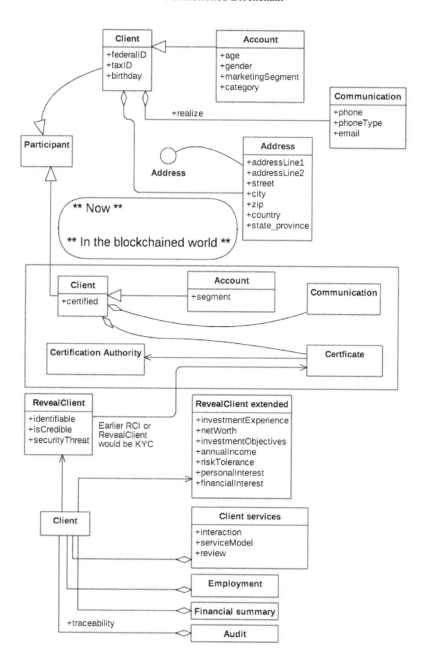

Figure 2 - Client Information

Think for a second on what the social networking sites offer. Certainly, they do not reveal what the world thinks of a person as their focus provides a mirror of the person's vanity - what the person thinks of his or her character. That does not help the planner, lender or employer. What the world thinks of someone makes that person easier to be identified, more credible and less of a threat. In a world where 'trust' matters, reviews from others are more effective in adding to that 'trust'. There is always a fine balance between anonymity and identity, which a peer review cannot eliminate. Certificates can ascertain, even verify, they cannot stop a threat or a crime. Being identified by TSA as a 'known traveler' can lower the risk of a threat, not clear the risk.

In the new frontiers of blockchain-ed permissioned networks and smart contracts, comes a whole new set of policies that define the roles and their rules of engagement in this new world.

Going deeper into understanding the Hyperledger set of tools, how they work, and how to model the financial planning network, we cover four notable offerings from Hyperledger – Fabric, Compose, Sawtooth and Burrow. The appeal of Hyperledger Fabric and Hyperledger Sawtooth-Burrow Ethereum Virtual Machine gives you the ability to run digitized policies on top of the block structure, without the need for coin and currency in such a midst. You can think of Bitcoin and currencies as yet another set of applications running on blockchain, just as the financial smart contracts. Their use-cases differ and throughout the book, our borders stay constrained by non-currency, permissioned blockchains.

The data within the blockchain structure is an ordered, back-linked list of blocks of transactions. Within the service, the blockchain comprising thousands of transactions stay persisted. With coin currency such as Bitcoin, the core client stores the blockchain metadata using Google's LevelDB[3] database, while Hyperledger Fabric uses Apache's CouchDB[4] and Sawtooth uses LMDB[5].

Blocks contain *"back"* links, each referring to the earlier block in the chain. Identification of each block within the blockchain comes from a hash, generated by a cryptographic hash algorithm[6] on the header of the block. Each block also references an earlier block, known as the parent block, through the *"preceding block hash"* field in the block header. Each block, consequently, holds the hash of its parent inside its own header. The sequence of hashes linking each block to its parent creates an upward chain going all the way back to the exact first block, known as the *"genesis"* block.

Inside the blockchain, a block works as a container, having a well-defined data structure that aggregates transactions meant for the ledger. Every block has a header and metadata, followed by the long list of transactions that make up the bulk. Block header is 80-bytes, while the average transaction measures around 250-bytes and the average block can contain over 500-transactions.

---

[3] https://github.com/google/leveldb
[4] http://couchdb.apache.org/
[5] https://github.com/LMDB
[6] In contrast to encryption, hashing is a one-way conversion. There is no provision for decryption. Hash values are comparable only.

The financial portfolio advisory system using Hyperledger components provides practical advice in protecting assets as part of a comprehensive wealth management plan; the bulk of transactions stored in distributed ledgers are shielded through cryptography and blockchain technology. It includes provisions to coordinate many strategies to protect assets such as the client's estate, investment management, retirement and business. Of course, several such services may be external to the blockchain architecture and invoked from the application. That makes the ecosystem, vibrant.

! With United States and EU mandating stronger checks on privacy and sensitive data being stowed in public databases, the architecture avoids all pitfalls of sharing any information other than cryptographic certificates. I built this application architecture around planning and needs of customers in need of wealth management. Investment allocations, life expectancy, recommendations and expected outcome make up this architecture. A client or customer, modeled in the wealth management scenario moves up the chain from being identifiable through a government issued or federally accepted token to an authorized certificate. The resulting strategy safeguards the person and assets from physical and legal risks and provides an effective way to keep financial planning on track. In maintaining such immutable, historical data, possible through blockchain; it gives the client the ability to weather any financial surprises.

Regulatory requirements ask for a deeper insight into clients and planners before admitting them into the business network.

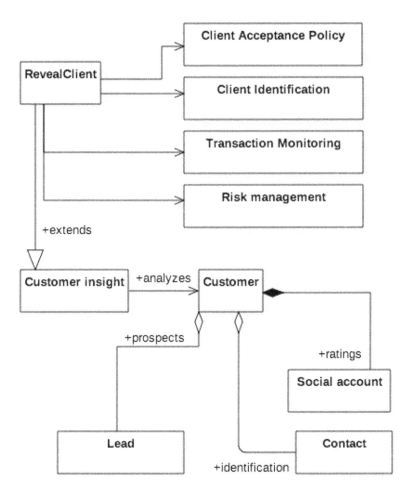

Figure 3 – An UML model to reveal the client and get insights

Client interactions

The UML class diagram (*as in figure 4*) shows the potential touch points where blockchain database fits in. The coin currency is presented as another investment; another application of blockchain, and an alternative means to making payments or increase savings.

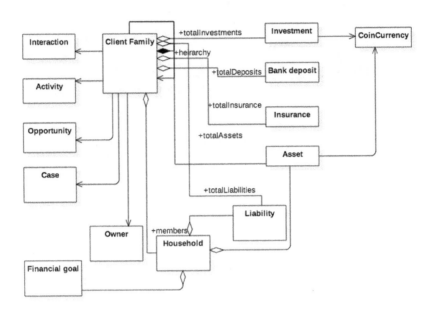

Figure 4 - Financial Planning Structure

Interactions, activities and opportunities resulting from advisory or exploratory events form a part of the routine that surround investments. The 'client family' comprises an owner and other members of the household. Not every member win access to the portfolio blockchain. Even if they do, their entitlements differ significantly from the owner. The portfolio harbors investments of different asset classes along with liabilities to suggest a well-rounded balance-sheet at any point of time.

Informing the client and gathering data

In the process of initiating a client or a customer, a remarkable amount of effort goes into gathering and sharing information, which can set the real tone in digitizing such material.

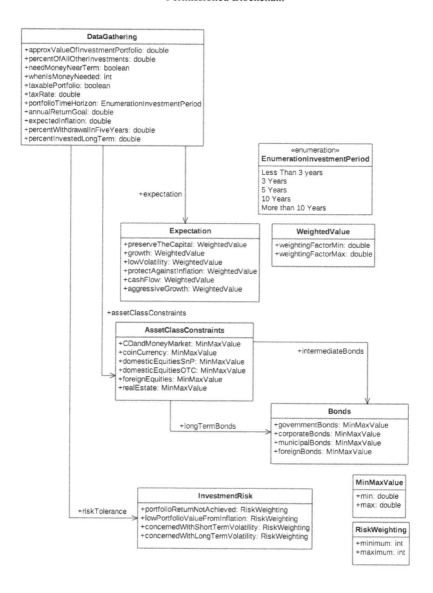

Figure 5 - Data Gathering

Informing the client while gathering data can come from human interactions or dealings through software media. Such conversational sessions are an important sign-off and can have a significant impact on the portfolio.

Constraints are an important aspect of data gathering. Knowing the constraints gives us an idea on how much the client is willing to invest, how much can he or she scatter the investments. Within the constraints lie the answers. Data gathering leads to a 'smart contract'. The design in Figure 6 captures the client's initial perspective of how the portfolio appears. As we progress through the making of the portfolio, the client's expectations, risks and concerns decrease or get elevated; the contract begins to serve as an ongoing checklist. Coin Currencies besides offering the ability to 'pay' also offers rewards, where a digital coin can get minted as part of the portfolio. Policies are the key to success in meeting the client's goals. Intrinsically, policies come about through an iterative process undergoing many modifications with lapses in time.

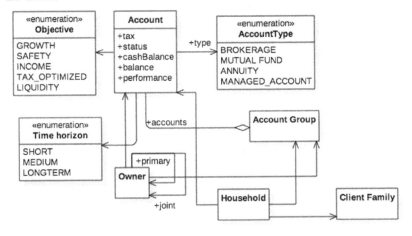

Figure 6 - Account Management

Portfolio account comprises the owner (*single account holder or joint*) along with the household. It maintains within its folds, the objectives and terms of investment as necessary. Other financial planning systems may want to group the accounts logically under different criteria like owner or household.

Account Management

The financial advisory system trudges along with the client to work its way through several evaluations. It starts with the process of selecting suitable goals and setting up a financial-account or multiple such accounts catering to these goals. See figure 6 on account management.

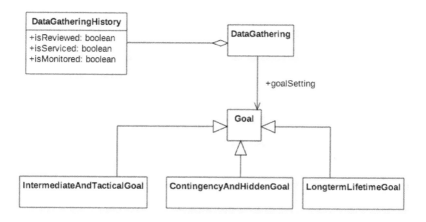

Figure 7 - Client review of plan and model

Client Review of Financial Plan and Model

What is needed by the system is the client's buy-in into an implementation which may well be laced with his or her appetite for risk. Goals can only be real if the constraints are known upfront, but that is not what humans are known to be good at. Therefore, the data gathering. Hence, the process of determining the different goal types and ensuring the client understands that the system is meant to address his or her concerns on the goals by knowing the constraints and expectations.

Client needs help with goals

I have no reasons to downplay the fact that setting a pragmatic goal is an integral part of the financial planning process. While every goal-set is a mix bag, not every client can foresee its value at the onset. It is more practical to let a third party such as the system suggest what makes a composite goal. Some time-tested strategies that worked before, will presumably continue to work in the new age - Intermediate or tactical goals comprise expenses and borrowings like college funds, education, weddings, recreation homes and vehicles. Such tactical goals are heavily constrained, as Harold Evensky describes them, "constraints are the three-cardinal system of time, dollar and priority". It is often hard to juggle the goals with even two of them. Strategic or lifetime goals plan for financial independence and retirement. Few clients may need cash flow for a few months, some for years, a small number may expect disability and life insurance, others may not. Contingent goals are what they are – unknown but occur at an unexpected time. Therefore, a few investments in insurance become essential. Fire, floods, accidents, loss of income are but a few in this category. Each different goal provisions for the withdrawals and amounts needed, the targeted savings for the withdrawals and the dates thereof. It is of no surprise that few people take advantage of this free and proven formula to success. In fact, Harvard Business School conducted a study on goal setting and found[7] that 83% of the population have no clearly defined goals. 14% have goals but poorly articulated. Only 3% have goals they commit to in writing. Figure 8 models the goal service in UML.

---

[7] Source – Financial Mentor

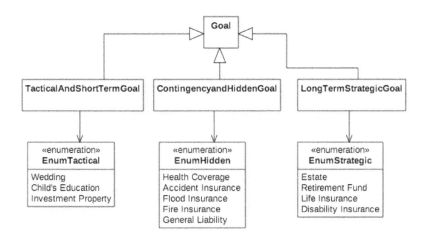

Figure 8 - Goal modeling class diagram

Four to five years is what a pragmatic plan can truly accommodate. Five years is the magic number, marking the end of an economy and the start of another. Any advisory system, worth its salt can charter a financial goal-setting worksheet to calculate the amount needed in savings to reach the goals. Savings goals can vary from short-term as under 3 years to medium-term, ranging between 3 to 10 years and long-term, beyond 10 years. What is required from any system is a continuous tab on the client's financial health. Not just wealth management issues and investments, but also the client's interests, values, motivations and concerns. Early on in planning cycle, the advisory system reviews all aspects of the client's financial undertakings. But priorities change over time and a person's life situation. Accounting for all the goals around financial independence, education, retirement income, improved cash flow, inheritance, estate taxes in the advisory plan and their inception or plan dates become useful in shaping the portfolio.

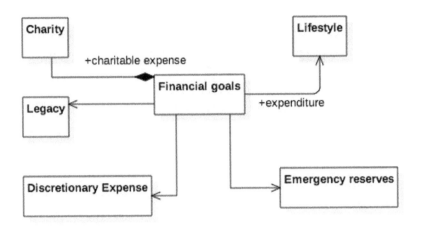

Figure 9 – Goals – core savings and excess

Often, a proposed financial plan may throw a scare, without the client expressing any discomfort. Though risk tolerance is unique to everyone, yet, people hide behind a mask and pretend to be risk averse. It is only when people open up to time and risk issues, optimizing the goal then for the client comes within easy reach. I repeat, any financial advisory system, worthy of respect, must offer the best conceivable solution along with some healthy alternatives to help the client define practical, measurable goals that can get added to the financial plan. The system must review the issues and challenges at each stage of the client's life and deliver strategies for handling changes in personal and financial circumstances. Besides, it must dive deep into financial and estate planning, pension, insurance and group benefits to recognize and tackle financial vulnerabilities. While mentoring the customer may not be the easiest when interacting with robotics or machines, newer systems are sprouting fast to add a human touch in redirecting the client's attention to other alternatives when the client refuses an option or is unwilling to take the coaching.

Challenging the investment is yet another area where machines fall short of being the most convincing contender. Educating and challenging is a human trait that often comes through story telling. It may still be hard to think how a machine could be imaginative, but it is clear, some algorithms will get "fuzzy" close.

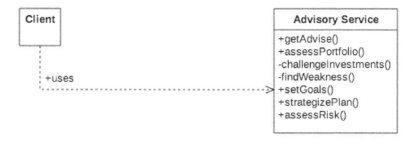

Figure 10 - Advisory Functions

On the subject of stories, a user's story of the requirements is the basis from which the architecture and engineering can proceed. User stories are a recognized way of capturing requirements. We can treat user stories as important development artifacts - as requirements expressed from the perspective of end-user goals. Often people refer to user stories as epics, themes or features but they all follow a comparable format. Think of a user story as a well-expressed set of requirements.

As a Portfolio Holder,	
I would like to set my goals, expectations and constraints, express my investments, justify the asset allocation, plan for retirement and financial independence. The system must justify the financial risks involved. Knowing my tax situation now and later would be of tremendous help. Incidentally, I would like to review the portfolio at my convenience and with no time constraints. I'd like my identity and the portfolio to remain secure and yet be able to work with the portfolio without the fear of threat or other hassles.	
Expected outcome:	A portfolio, I can monitor, any place, any time.
Failed outcome:	A portfolio that failed to meet the goals and expectations.

Knowing what is expected from the requirements, it is time to examine the prospects of designing a smart contract in both Hyperledger Fabric and Sawtooth. Realizing, the hammer can meet the nail in several unusual ways, our course of action starts with the Hyperledger Composer, from where we work our way into Sawtooth and inject Smart Contracts into different blockchain layers.

Installing Hyperledger Fabric and Composer

In order to run Hyperledger Fabric, the Docker community edition offers a rewarding preference. Once you understand how Hyperledger composer works, you will understand the amount of heavy lifting it does to build a blockchain application. You can install Hyperledger composer by using NPM, the Node-JS packaging manager. Please run a sanity check on the Node-JS version and if it is installed. It should be 8.x or higher. Between Linux Ubuntu 16.0.4 or macOS High Sierra, the installations have many commonalities.

Certifying MacOS

Activating "xcode" on your Mac is also a priority, if you are planning on using a Mac for development. As you will be running many commands from the command line, start a new terminal window on your local machine. On macOS, from within "Finder", select Applications, Utilities and Terminal. Once the terminal window comes up, run the command to install 'xcode' for MacOS.

```
$ xcode -select --install
```

Subsequent installation steps are common to macOS and Linux (Ubuntu 16.0.4). If Node-JS is missing in your development environment, basically download the node.js installer[8] from the node website and complete the installation process. Once complete, you can create a folder for Hyperledger Composer and install the CLI tools.

---

[8] https://nodejs.org/en/download/

Just a word of caution, if you have been using Fabric 1.1 or earlier versions, please uninstall the Composer CLI from before and destroy and purge any prior Hyperledger Fabric Docker images.

```
$ npm install -g composer-cli
$ npm install -g composer-rest-server
$ npm install -g generator-hyperledger-composer
$ npm install -g yo
$ npm install -g composer-playground
```

From the above list, it is apparent, there are several tools involved. Hyperledger Composer generator along with Yeoman gives you the head wind to kick-start the software application by creating the right folders and sample code. The scripts above complete the Composer toolset, installing Hyperledger Fabric comes next. It requires downloading the fabric tools and setting up the Docker environment to house the installation. In a directory of choice, assuming the directory is ~/fabric-tools, download the archive file containing the tools to install and run Hyperledger Fabric[9].

```
$ mkdir ~/fabric-tools
$ cd ~/fabric-tools
```

The next action fetches fabric files from GitHub to the 'fabric-tools' folder. Even though Windows 10 offers 'curl' as a beta function at the time of writing, the command will not work with Windows. You are better off using the browser to download the files[10].

---

[9] https://hyperledger.github.io/composer/unstable/installing/development-tools.html
[10] https://github.com/hyperledger/composer-tools/tree/master/packages/fabric-dev-servers

```
$ curl -O
https://raw.githubusercontent.com/hyperledger/composer-
tools/master/packages/fabric-dev-servers/fabric-dev-servers.tar.gz
$ tar -xvf fabric-dev-servers.tar.gz
$ cd ~/fabric-tools
$ export FABRIC_VERSION=hlfv11
$ ./downloadFabric.sh
```

Now that you have a local copy of Fabric on your computer, you can continue to install with the command *docker-compose* to download and populate the Docker containers. Incidentally, Docker also has a module named compose, not to confuse with Hyperledger's composer. The next set of scripts starts the containers for Fabric.

```
$ cd ~/fabric-tools
$ export FABRIC_VERSION=hlfv11
// uninstall the older Hyperledger composer version
$ npm uninstall composer@0.18.2
$ npm install -g composer-cli@0.19
$ ./startFabric.sh
```

The response you get on your console will probably resemble the output below.

```
...
ARCH=$ARCH docker-compose -f
"${DIR}"/composer/docker-compose.yml up -d
Creating network "composer_default" with the default
driver
Creating orderer.example.com ... done
Creating couchdb              ... done
Creating ca.org1.example.com    ... done
Creating peer0.org1.example.com ... done

# wait for Hyperledger Fabric to start
...
```

Though the Hyperledger fabric documentation recommends starting with a Peer Admin account, I would defer that to a few more steps. If the Peer Admin card creation goes with no issues, then by all means run the command below. In Hyperledger Fabric, *peers* enforce the concepts of administrators, members or users. Peer command has five other sub-commands, each of which allows administrators to carry out a specific set of tasks related to a peer. For example, you can use the ***peer channel*** sub-command to join a peer to a channel, or the "***Peer Chaincode***" command to deploy a smart contract *Chaincode* to a peer. Administrators have permission to install Hyperledger *Fabric Chaincode*[11] for a new business network onto peers. Members do not have permission to install *Chaincode*.

In deploying a business network to a set of peers, the user must offer an administrative identity to all the peers. A peer administrative business network card ensures the identities of administrator and readiness of certificates. As such, a certificate and private key must be generated and associated with the peer admin identity. Hyperledger Composer provides a sample Hyperledger Fabric network, where the peer administrator for this network is ***PeerAdmin***, and the available scripts easily imports the identity into the network.

Deploying a business network to Hyperledger Fabric, requires a bootstrap registrar to manage its internal certificate authority.

---

[11] Chaincode is a software program, written in Go that implements a prescribed interface. Chaincode runs in a secured Docker container isolated from the endorsing peer process. Chaincode initializes and manages ledger state through transactions submitted by applications

The Hyperledger Composer development environment contains a pre-configured instance of Hyperledger Fabric with a specific enrollment identity and secret for the bootstrap registrar. We can use the pre-configured identity to run our financial planning example or create a new registrar. When the Hyperledger Composer starts, it routinely generates one business network administrator participant. The identity used in deploying the business network stays assigned to that business network administrator participant, such that one may use the identity to interact with the business network after deployment. Hyperledger Fabric peer administrators may not have permission to issue new identities using the Hyperledger Fabric Certificate Authority. This may restrict the ability of the business network administrator to on-board other participants from their organization. It may be prudent to offer permissions in issuing new identities using the Certificate Authority in the earlier stages of assembling the network. One can exercise additional options along with the "composer network start" command to specify the business network administrators required for the business network deployment.

The script below creates the Composer Peer Admin Card.

```
$ ./createPeerAdminCard.sh
```

With Fabric running and the peer admin card generated, the focus changes to the financial planning application contract and network design.

Design

Foremost, we must define and build a permission'd network - a network made of the client, an advisory system and reviewer. A business network definition has a file layout analogous to the one described beneath.

```
models/
lib/
permissions.acl
package.json
README.md
```

On a different terminal window, focus your attention on running *Yeoman,* which incidentally, commences the network[12]. I would at this juncture spend a few minutes in answering these questions.

What is the use-case all about?
What name would I give to the business network?
Who is the author and what is his/her email?
What is the namespace to be used in the network?

Giving a proper business network name is all about the right semantics. I have suggested a very generic name. In a real application, proper naming and descriptions go a long way.

---

[12] http://yeoman.io/generators/

The namespace comes next. A proper namespace maintains the focus in the midst of many types of networks. The namespace allows similar functionality to exist in different namespaces. Hyperledger-composer uses Yeoman to generate the preliminary card assembly and a sample model.

```
$ yo hyperledger-composer
```

From the menu that emerges in the prompt, select Business Network. More prompts appear to define the network, a sample model and a folder structure.

```
Welcome to the Hyperledger Composer project generator
? Please select the type of project: Business Network
You can run this generator using: 'yo hyperledger-
composer:businessnetwork'
Welcome to the business network generator
? Business network name: financial-plan
? Description: Financial Planning
? Author name:  Dev B
? Author email: devb@linux.com
? License: Apache-2.0
? Namespace: com.devb.wm
   create index.js
   …
   create README.md
```

This generates a skeleton business network with an asset,  participant and transaction, as well as a mocha unit test code. You may use the 'composer archive create' utility to generate a business network archive from the contents of such a directory. A smart contract file is normally found in the 'model/' folder created by Yeoman. It goes by the extension '.cto' and begins with the *name-space* declared by you when you ran Yeoman.

```
namespace com.devb.wm
```

The namespace, per se has much less to do with the network but it's re-use in different networks ensures the uniqueness of all resources in that model and even if different resources have the same name, the namespace sets them apart uniquely.

```
concept Allocation {
  o Double moneyMarket
  o Double bonds
  o Double stock
  o Double insurance
  o Double realEstate
}
```

In the next few paragraphs, I shall describe the objects and components as they logically occur. In financial planning, "allocation" is a "concept" where the investment amount is distributed to money market, bonds, stocks, insurance and real estate through different mathematic models which we will discuss in the latter part of this chapter. Hyperledger composer comes with a pre-packaged, vocabulary of terms, where "concept" resembles a UML class. In the model, permitted is the use of "*concepts*" just the way UML classes support a participant, asset or transaction type. The concepts and other structures are held by braces supporting the "*attributes*" within. Attributes within the concept can use pre-defined types like String, Double, Integer and types defined or used within the model.

Example:

```
                                        Composer

concept Percent {
  o Double amount
}
```

Attributes and references start with a prefix. When prefixed by 'o', it specifies an object and '-->' identifies an object by reference. A data-type such as "String" is a UTF8 encoded String, Double is a double precision 64-bit numeric value, Integer is a 32-bit signed whole number, Long is a 64-bit signed whole number, DateTime is an ISO-8601 compatible time instance, with optional time zone and UTZ offset; and Boolean is either true or false.

The model file is the template for the smart contract. Resources in the CTO file can range from Abstract types, Assets, Participants, Transactions and Events. Besides resources can be 'Enumerated Types' and 'Concepts'. A key field is not associated with a concept because concepts are not stored in registries, and their presence cannot be referenced in other relationships. Incidentally, attributes can have 'default' values, they can be 'optional' and offer 'ranges'. Using REGEX definitions to format the data type and control the data definition is an added feature. Resources and their properties may also have decorators attached. Decorators find use in annotating the model with metadata.

In the financial planning model, 'rainy day' or hidden goals are not explicit goals, they are more contingency - like an unfortunate, unforeseen auto accident. Intermediate are those with finite time objectives like college-education and wedding. Lifetime goals suggest the idea of retirement.

Composer

```
concept Goals {
  o String clientId
  o Allocation rainyDay
  o Allocation intermediate
  o Allocation lifetime
  o Percent basicLivingExpenses
  o Percent fixedTerminalExpenses
  o Percent inflatableExpenses
}
```

Constraints are the client's aversion to risk. Keeping a safe percent of investments in cash is probably the client's safety net.

```
concept Constraints {
  o String clientId
  o Percent liquidity
  o Percent marketability
  o String threshold
}
```

Investment is about building an ecosystem where money is generated as part of the process. Expectations come from such investments and cash flows generated from them help meet the client's livelihood.

```
concept Expectations {
  o String clientId
  o Double cashFlowBonds
  o Double cashFlowStock
  o Double cashReserve
}
```

Both market and cash flow projections must consider any anticipated inflation and in doing so, forecast the projected portfolio value.

```
concept Projections {
  o String clientId
  o Double anticipatedCashFlow
  o Double anticipatedInflation
  o Double anticipatedPortfolioValue
  o Percent chanceSuccess
}
```

To capture the different parties and clients, enumerated are the different client types. Included in that list is the 'Trust' or 'Trustee'.

```
enum ClientType {
  o INDIVIDUAL
  o PARTY
  o TRUST
  o POWEROFATTORNEY
}
```

Expression of a client or customer comes from an id. As explained earlier, the public cryptographic key or a PEM file could well be the only identifier needed for the client.

```
participant Client identified by clientId {
  o String clientId
  o ClientType clientType
  o String firstname
  o String midInitials optional
  o String lastname
  o String publicKey
}

enum AssetType {
  o ASSET
  o LIABILITY
}

asset Investment identified by assetId {
  o String assetId
  o String assetGroup
  o String assetClass
```

```
  o String assetSummary
  o String taxJurisdiction
  o String currency
  o AssetType
  o Double value
  o Double projectedValue
  o Double interest
  o Double dividends
  o Double capitalGains
}
```

In the area of estate planning and management, provisions for distribution and directions are sustained within the asset.

```
asset Estate identified by assetId {
  o String assetId
  o String distributionUponDeath
  o Double value
  o Double estateTaxes
  o Double probateFees
  o String directionsForDisburtion
}
```

The enumeration data-type of 'Recurring Basis' has its usage with premium payments as they occur. Several premiums occur every day; many of them annually.

```
enum RecurringBasis {
  o DAILY
  o WEEKLY
  o MONTHLY
  o QUARTERLY
  o ANNUAL
  o ONETIMEONLY
}
```

Care, like estate planning provisions for elderly, child or disability that may occur in the future, necessitates a different set of investments.

```
Composer

concept Care {
  o String careId
  o String referenceNum
  o String description
  o Double cost
  o RecurringBasis basis
  o Double monthlyPremium
  o DateTime expirationDate
}

concept Insurance {
  o String insuranceId
  o String referenceNum
  o String description
  o String insuranceType
  o Double value
  o RecurringBasis basis
  o Double premium
  o DateTime expirationDate
}
```

A divorce plan is just another contingency and like 'care' or 'insurance' may not even apply to the client. The reader will notice, they become optional in the portfolio.

```
concept DivorcePlan {
  o String divorcePlanId
  o String referenceNum
  o String description
  o DateTime expirationDate
}
```

The portfolio has a status-lifecycle. Initially, the portfolio stays dormant in a de-activated state, and then activated or merged with another at a later stage.

```
                                              Composer

enum PortfolioStatus {
  o ACTIVATE
  o DEACTIVATE
  o MERGE
}

asset Portfolio identified by portfolioId {
  o String portfolioId
  --> Investment[] investments
  --> Client[] clients
  --> Estate[] estates
  o Boolean reviewed
  o Goals goals optional
  o Constraints constraints optional
  o Expectations expectations optional
  o Projections projections optional
  o String[] disclosures optional
  o Care[] care optional
  o Insurance[] insurances optional
  o DivorcePlan[] divorcePlans optional
}
```

Composer allows you to declare any data-type in the model as an array using the [] notation. Care, Insurance and Divorce plans often occur as multiple investments and consequently expressed as arrays.

```
                                    Composer

enum AccountStatus {
  o ACTIVE
  o INACTIVE
  o DORMANT
}

asset Account identified by accountId {
  o String accountId
  o AccountStatus status
  o Client client
  o Portfolio[] portfolio optional
  o String[] Notes optional
  o DateTime beginningDate
}
```

Transactions are operations within a contract that result as entries in the ledger. By definition, the primary aim of a ledger is to ease the assets between people. Many such transactions are stored in pockets of blocks in a blockchain.

```
                                    Composer

transaction SetGoals {
  --> Client client
  --> Investment investment
  o Goals goals optional
  o Constraints constraints optional
  o Expectations expectations optional
  o Projections projections optional
}
transaction Optimize {
  --> Portfolio portfolio
}
transaction ModifyPortfolio {
  --> Portfolio portfolio
  o Allocation newAllocation
}
```

```
event ChangeAccount {
  --> Client client
  --> Portfolio portfolio
}

event ChangePortfolioValue {
  --> Portfolio portfolio
  o Double oldValue
  o Double newValue
}

transaction ClientReview {
  --> Portfolio portfolio
  o Boolean review
  o Boolean machineReview
}
```

This calls for implementation of separate functional logic for each of the transactions declared in the 'lib' folder. The model file just declares the transaction, it does not tell Fabric or Composer what must go in there. Thus, the need for a separate JavaScript file. All transactions – their internal workings go into the logic.js. Think of the contract as made of two different parts – first, the declarative structure and the second, transactional behavior. Since transactions involve participants and assets, the JavaScript code fetches participants from their registry, assets from their registry and complete the contract between them. You will notice that such is the case with the client review function and changing the portfolio value.

Every transaction on successful completion and consensus gets lodged in blocks within the blockchain, enriching the ledger with pertinent historical data on 'who said what, who did what' within the network.

We must also plan for security and access control upfront and not as an after-thought. A *participants.acl* file controls the participants and provides them with authorized access into the network and the resources within. Rules can be coarse or fine grained depending on the participants and type of transactions.

```
                                              Composer
rule EverybodyCanReadEverything {
    description: "Allow participants read access to resources"
    participant: "com.devb.wm.Person"
    operation: READ
    resource: "com.devb.wm.*"
    action: ALLOW
}

rule EverybodyCanSubmitTransactions {
    description: "Allow participants to submit transactions"
    participant: "com.devb.wm.Person"
    operation: CREATE
    resource: "com.devb.wm.*"
    action: ALLOW
}
rule OwnerHasFullAccessToTheirAssets {
    description: "Allow participants full access to assets"
    participant(p): "com.devb.wm.Person"
    operation: ALL
    resource(r): "com.devb.wm.PropertyHome"
    condition: (r.owner.getIdentifier() ===
                p.getIdentifier())
    action: ALLOW
}

rule SystemACL {
    description:   "System ACL to permit all access"
    participant:
    "org.hyperledger.composer.system.Participant"
    operation: ALL
    resource: "org.hyperledger.composer.system.**"
    action: ALLOW
}
```

```
rule NetworkAdminUser {
    description: "Grant biz network admin access to user resources"
    participant:
    "org.hyperledger.composer.system.NetworkAdmin"
    operation: ALL
    resource: "**"
    action: ALLOW
}

rule NetworkAdminSystem {
    description: "Grant biz network admin access to system res"
    participant:
    "org.hyperledger.composer.system.NetworkAdmin"
    operation: ALL
    resource: "org.hyperledger.composer.system.**"
    action: ALLOW
}
```

A connection profile provides the required configuration to attach to Hyperledger Fabric. One can save it as JSON by the name *connection.json*. The x-type declared within formulates the access to a certain Fabric version. It could be "hlfv1" or "hlfv11. If you are using the certification authority provided by Fabric, the *connection.json* is the correct way to go.

```
{"name": "fabric-network",
   "x-type": "hlfv11", "version": "1.0.0",
   "peers": {
      "peer0.org1.example.com": {
      "url": "grpc://localhost:7051",
      "eventUrl": "grpc://localhost:7053"}
   },
```

```json
"certificateAuthorities": {
  "ca.org1.example.com": {
  "url": "http://localhost:7054",
  "caName": "ca.org1.example.com"}},
"orderers": {
  "orderer.example.com":
    {"url": "grpc://localhost:7050"}
},
"organizations": {
  "Org1": {
  "mspid": "Org1MSP",
  "peers": ["peer0.org1.example.com"],
  "certificateAuthorities":
    ["ca.org1.example.com"]}
},
"channels": {
  "composerchannel": {
  "orderers": ["orderer.example.com"],
  "peers": {"peer0.org1.example.com": {
    "endorsingPeer": true,
    "chaincodeQuery": true,
    "eventSource": true}}
  }
},
"client": {
  "organization": "Org1",
  "connection": {
  "timeout": {"peer":
    {"endorser": "300",
  "eventHub": "300",
  "eventReg": "300" },
  "orderer": "300"}
  }
}
}
```

As part of the next steps, we must generate a Network Card using either a certificate, or user id and password. Compare this to an access card that's needed to enter a controlled and monitored physical building or premises. This network access card is similar in concept, except it is virtual.

```
$ cd financial-plan
$ composer card create --file fp.card --businessNetworkName
financial-planning --connectionProfileFile connection.json --user
financialadvisor --enrollSecret secret
```

Hyperledger composer has a unique bundling process where all artifacts come together as an archive. Generating the network archive is next in our list of activities. The network archive gives you the flexibility of distributing the application to different peers and nodes. Later, when modifications come in and the model moves through its lifecycle of changes, newer archive versions take their place.

```
$ cd financial-plan
$ composer archive create --sourceType dir --sourceName . -a
financial-planning.bna
```

The system responds with results as below in generating the file *financial-planning.bna* (*business network archive*).

```
Creating Business Network Archive
Looking for package.json of Business Network Definition
Input directory:
/Users/[folder]/Blockchain/h-composer/financial-plan
Found:
        Description: Financial Planning
        Name: financial-plan
        Identifier: financial-plan@0.0.1
    Written Business Network Definition Archive file to
        Output file: financial-planning.bna
Command succeeded
```

Once the archive is generated, it is ready to be deployed to the running instance of Hyperledger Fabric.

```
$ composer network start -a financial-planning.bna -A
financialadvisor -S secret -c fp.card -f financialadvisor@fp
```

If the above command fails to succeed, you may resort to using the pre-bundled sample card as a fallback.

```
$ composer runtime install –card PeerAdmin@hlfv1 --
businessNetworkName financial-planning
```

```
      Installing runtime for business network
financial-planning. This may take a minute...
Command succeeded
```

And deploy the Network Card.

```
$ composer network start --card PeerAdmin@hlfv1 --
networkAdmin admin --networkAdminEnrollSecret adminpw --
archiveFile financial-plan@0.0.1 --file fp.card
```

Now, when you start the REST server, you have access to the network, contract and blockchain.

```
$ composer-rest-server
```

```
When prompted, enter the name admin@financial-
planning
```

The composer rest server comes along with a client through which you can invoke the operations. The Node.JS middleware running at port 3000 is accessible through http://localhost:3000/explorer.

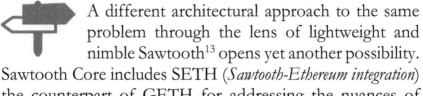 A different architectural approach to the same problem through the lens of lightweight and nimble Sawtooth[13] opens yet another possibility. Sawtooth Core includes SETH (*Sawtooth-Ethereum integration*) the counterpart of GETH for addressing the nuances of Ethereum Virtual Machine. Seth also makes it easy to port existing EVM smart contracts and DApps[14].

In the Sawtooth world, the Smart Contract is akin to Transaction Families. Seth has three components, client, transaction processor and the RPC server. The "seth-rpc" server is an HTTP server that acts as an adapter between the Ethereum JSON RPC API and the client interface provided by Sawtooth. Sawtooth's Seth is Hyperledger Sawtooth and Burrow running the Ethereum Virtual Machine enabling Solidity created Smart Contracts to run in that environment. The Seth client is the user-facing CLI tool for interacting with a Sawtooth-Seth network.

You have several options for Sawtooth installation - Docker for macOS in newer machines, Docker with VBOX macOS for older machines, Ubuntu Xenial 16.0.4 and AWS Ubuntu instance. While the installation hovers around Sawtooth-Seth and Hyperledger-Composer for Fabric, it also includes Truffle for Sawtooth-Burrow instance. The (-g) or global parameter is optional. You always have a choice of housekeeping with NPM. You can keep the installation local and not provide the global parameter.

---

[13] https://sawtooth.hyperledger.org/docs/
[14] https://www.coindesk.com/information/what-is-a-decentralized-application-dapp/

While you are at it, you may also want to install the Solidity[15] compiler and Truffle[16] through NPM. Truffle provides an elegant way of compiling and deploying Smart Contracts into EVM running over Blockchain data. Web3 library is required by Truffle to run Smart Contracts on Sawtooth-Seth.

```
$ npm install -g truffle
$ npm install -g solc
$ npm install -g web3
```

Docker Community Edition[17] for Mac is what you need for installation. Docker CE for Mac is an easy-to-install desktop application for building, debugging, and testing Dockerized apps on a Mac. It runs integrated Docker platform and tools, Docker command line, Docker Compose, and Docker Notary. The installation can only proceed with Apple Mac OS Yosemite 10.10.3 or above. If you have an older version of Mac (either Hardware or OS version), you will certainly need the Docker Toolbox. Simply download Docker and install the software. Also, confirm you have provisioned at least 4GB RAM for the VM.

The instructions below for installing Docker are for Ubuntu only.

```
$ sudo apt-get update
$ sudo apt-get install apt-transport-https |
ca-certificates curl software-properties-common
$ curl -fsSL | https://download.docker.com/linux/ubuntu/gpg
    | $ sudo apt-key add -
```

---

[15] http://solidity.readthedocs.io/en/develop/index.html
[16] http://truffleframework.com/
[17] https://store.docker.com/editions/community/docker-ce-desktop-mac

Verify the Docker installation.

```
$ sudo apt-key fingerprint 0EBFCD88
$ sudo add-apt-repository "deb [arch=amd64] \
https://download.docker.com/linux/ubuntu \
   $(lsb_release -cs) stable"
$ sudo apt-get update
$ sudo apt-get install docker-ce
```

For Ubuntu, you will also need ***docker-compose,*** which is a separate installation.

```
$ sudo curl -L |
https://github.com/docker/compose/releases/download/1.20.1/doc
ker-compose-`uname -s`-`uname -m` -o /usr/local/bin/docker-
compose
$ sudo chmod +x /usr/local/bin/docker-compose
```

Verify the docker-compose copy.

```
$ docker-compose --version
```

After the installation, on a separate terminal, or if you are using VS-Code, use the integrated terminal and check the Docker instance.

```
$ docker run hello-world
```

If the "hello world" appears on the console among other messages, you can breathe easy – considering another installation completed. Try another test just to confirm.

```
$ docker ps
```

The command, 'docker ps' will list all the containers running on the local computer. If your Mac did not come with HomeBrew[18], you will undeniably need it to install a whole range of things necessary to run Sawtooth-Seth and other items.

```
$ /usr/bin/ruby -e "$(curl -fsSL
https://raw.githubusercontent.com/Homebrew/install/master/install)"
```

You will also need 'git[19]' client to fetch code from GitHub. Moving on to installing Sawtooth-Seth, I will walk you through several steps to ensure you have the right tools at your disposal.

```
$ git clone \ https://github.com/hyperledger/sawtooth-seth
$ cd sawtooth-seth
$ docker-compose up --build
```

The last command calls for a decent coffee break. The build lasts a while. I trust you had assigned four gigabytes of VRAM for the docker instance. If the installation fails, simply increase the RAM size and start all over again. Once the Docker containers are up and running, it makes perfect sense to check them again.

```
$ docker ps
```

You will see a few container instances of Seth and Sawtooth running. Now you can run a few tests. Open the browser and then type 'http://localhost:8080/blocks'.

---

[18] https://brew.sh/
[19] https://git-scm.com/download

If you receive a JSON response reporting on the blocks used up in the Blockchain, you can be assured Sawtooth is up and running. Sawtooth REST API Server uses port 8080, 3030 stays captured by the Seth-RPC Server. If you are using a cloud instance – AWS EC2 or Azure, please keep those ports accessible. You may now try your hand at *"**shelling**"* into one such container and running blockchain transactions within.   Incidentally, you do not have to rebuild the containers every time you fire up Sawtooth.

```
$ cd sawtooth-seth
$ docker-compose up
```

```
...
Starting sawtooth-validator ... done
Starting seth-tp            ... done
Starting seth-rpc           ... done
Starting block-info-tp      ... done
Starting settings-tp        ... done
Starting rest-api           ... done
Starting seth-cli           ... done
Attaching to sawtooth-validator, block-info-tp, seth-
tp, rest-api, seth-rpc, settings-tp, seth-cli
...
```

```
$ docker exec -it seth-rpc bash
```

While you are transported into the **seth-rpc** container, you are confronted with completely new surroundings where you appear as root. *"**seth-rpc**"* container lets the CLI run transactions that are involved with smart contracts. Since all transactions accessible through its RPC interface are required to come from a verified and certified source, the first thing within the Docker shell is to generate a PEM file that holds the credentials. The command below generates a new, password-encrypted key.

```
$ openssl ecparam -genkey -name secp256k1 | openssl ec -out
alias.pem -aes128
```

The newly generated '*alias.pem*' file is quite unique. Assign this public encrypted file to an 'alias'. Interacting with Seth, requires us to create an account on the network. This account is associated with the new private key. You can use any encryption cipher by changing the final -aes128 flag or omitting the flag to generate the key.

Examples of different ciphers are AES128, AES256, AES (cipher suites using 128-bit AES, 256-bit AES or either 128 or 256-bit AES), ARIA128, ARIA256, ARIA (cipher suites using 128-bit ARIA, 256-bit ARIA or either 128 or 256-bit ARIA), SHA256, SHA384 (cipher suites using SHA256 or SHA384) or MD5 to name a few. Dropping the flag disables the encryption.

```
$ seth account import alias.pem alias
```

Hence, you open an account with the credentials and assign to a variable '*alias*'; the alias name could be anything alias1 or myalias. It stays unique to this account. Copying the key to an internal directory and creating an alias for the key makes the key reference-able for future commands. What remains in completing the account is accomplished by running the command '*seth command create*' and obtaining the address used by the process. In the Blockchain world, a nonce helps in generating a unique address where there are possibilities of conflicts.

```
seth account create --nonce=0 --wait alias
```

One thing I am sure that strikes you odd is the *"–wait"* instruction appended to the account creation command. The asynchronous wait ensures you receive an acknowledgment when the operation is complete. The response you receive may resemble the one below, the hash codes that appear may be different.

```
Transaction Receipt:  { "TransactionID":
"36140169f684da471acc4a75ced7e…",
 "Address": "659f1526b3a62a81039ab840d71eac5751370b36" }
```

The command should display the address of your brand-new account upon success of the command. Please store the *"address"* returned by the Transaction Receipt. The next step is an important and often forgotten or missed, which requires the account be unlocked. Shell into the *"seth-rpc"* container if you have not already and copy the PEM file to /root/.sawtooth/ folder and restart the server unlocking the alias(es).

Tip – Hyperledger Sawtooth documentation is not perfect. Much of seth-rpc setup came from my conversations with the folks working for Hyperledger Sawtooth. We went through a series of Jira tickets and iterations before we got this right.

```
$ docker exec -it seth-rpc bash
$ cp alias.pem /root/.sawtooth/
$ seth init http://rest-api:8008
$ seth-rpc --connect tcp://comp-seth-rpc:4004 --bind 0.0.0.0:3030
--unlock alias
```

Now you can test the API by posting the JSON.

```
{url: 'http://127.0.0.1:3030', method: 'POST',
json: {"jsonrpc": "2.0", "id": 19, "method": "eth_sendTransaction",
"params": [
    {"from": "0x90e77c172a....", "gas": "0x6691b7",
    "gasPrice": "0x174876e800", "data":5260200160....
}
```

When the **seth-rpc** server restarts after unlocking the alias, or series of aliases (*alias1, alias2, alias3*), it opens the access to the account from external sources like a Node-JS application or truffle to post contracts or run their methods.

```
$ seth show account [Address]
```

In this example it would be a **seth show** command as illustrated. It would return the contents of the transaction referred by the address.

```
$ seth show account
659f1526b3a62a81039ab840d71eac5751370b36
```

The syntax of a Smart Contract for SETH comes from Solidity[20]. It has an Object-Oriented flavor where the term contract encapsulates a UML class. It is left to us to declare and realize the attributes and operations within the body of the contract. In the lines of financial planning, I introduce a simple portfolio design for SETH. We can now use Truffle[21] to compile and deploy the contract. To begin with, we create a separate folder and run the truffle command to initialize the smart contract design.

```
$ truffle init
```

---

[20] https://github.com/ethereum/solidity

[21] http://truffleframework.com/

 Truffle like Yeoman initializes the folder by creating a few sub-folders and necessary code. In one of the sub-folders *'contracts'*, you will find a *'Migrations.sol'* pre-populated by Truffle. Our contract, *'Portfolio.sol'* will reside alongside it.

```solidity
pragma solidity ^0.4.17;
contract Portfolio {
    struct Client {
        uint investing;
        bool isInvested;
        bool isIdentified;
        InvestmentAsset inasset;
    }
    struct InvestmentAsset {
        uint stockId;
        bytes32 name;
        uint number;
        uint marketValue;
    }
    mapping(address => Client) public client;
    InvestmentAsset[] public investment;
    function invest(uint stockId) public
    returns (bool) { Client storage investor =
            client[msg.sender];
        require(!investor.isInvested);
        require(investor.isIdentified);
        investor.isInvested = true;
        investor.inasset = investment[stockId];
        return true;
    }
}
```

The code written in *Solidity* declares a client, an investment asset and a function that conjoins the client to the investment. Truffle achieves in transporting the code to Sawtooth-Burrow running on Docker containers. In most cases, a good practice is in keeping the Solidity code small and breaking the Smart Contract into smaller chunks to avoid large 'gas' usage. With Sawtooth-Seth, 'gas' prices and consumption do not matter as software and hardware expenses carry no price value but controlled through network permission-ing. To execute this code, we will need the 'Address' as shown to us before. Truffle needs to know it will no longer communicate with 'Ganache' – its own Blockchain implementation, but with Sawtooth-Burrow.

 The folder used in truffle initialization has a file called "truffle.js". Please alter this file and validate it points to the Sawtooth instance.

```
const Web3 = require('web3');
const web3 = new Web3(new Web3.providers.HttpProvider(
        'http://127.0.0.1:3030/'));
module.exports = {
  networks: {
   'sawtooth': {
     network_id: '19',
     host: '127.0.0.1' ,
       // address of the alias
     from: '659f1526b3a62a81039ab840d71eac5751370b36',
     port: 3030
   }
  }
}
```

Truffle requires the Web3 libraries to access **seth-rpc** running at port 3030. The 'from' parameter carries the address of the alias. Using proper configuration, we can use Truffle to compile and deploy the code to Sawtooth. You may receive an error when deploying. This customarily happens if the running node has no accounts. From its documentation, Truffle appears to deploy contracts using the first account available, the 'from' property in the 'configuration' ensures the framework works intimately with the account just generated.

```
$ truffle compile
$ truffle deploy --network sawtooth –reset
```

You may also use additional CLI parameters to obtain more information when deploying the contract.

```
$ truffle migrate --network sawtooth --reset --verbose-rpc
```

Just remember, you were doing all this outside the container. Within the confines of the container, things are different as we can use Seth to deploy any Smart Contracts to the running instance. To use Seth, let us return to the terminal window that had been opened using Docker Bash shell earlier. Within the Docker Container, you will install the "Solc" compiler and an editor, if the container instance does not provide them. I prefer the 'nano' editor over 'vim', but any choice of text-editor is personal and deferred to the reader. Since there is no room for graphics in the container, whatever editor you select must be a text-driven one.

```
# npm install -g solc
# apt-get update
# apt-get install nano
```

Edit and save the ***Portfolio.sol*** using the 'nano' editor or the editor of your choice within the container and run the solidity compiler against the file.

```
# solcjs Portfolio.sol –bin
```

Solidity creates a run-time file; whose contents appear as hex code. It is easy to 'cat' the generated hex file and copy it to the clipboard.

```
# cat Portfolio_sol_Portfolio.bin
```

You must copy the contents exactly as displayed to deploy the contract.

```
$ seth contract create --wait alias
606060405234156100000f57600080fd5b6102508061001e6000396
000f30060606040526004361061005757600035 7c01...
```

The system should prompt back with a notice that the contract created is ready for requests.

```
Contract created
Transaction Receipt:  { "TransactionID":
"45c0c3903faca0671e2eed8a3efe7d9afe9690088ca7d59b40b5e7
6793be85b12ca68a47fd584e99ed974db8f6d1fc8983241b3c24ae
37977b5c7f1f988cf8fa",
  "GasUsed": 21, "Address":
"46f7c50dd835ca3538c8e0302f9b3faf385f708d",
  "ReturnValue": "606060405..."
}
```

With the contract in place, it is time to create a JavaScript file and run it with Node-JS within the Docker Shell.

```
$ node abi-generator.js
```

```
let abi = require('ethereumjs-abi')
let newstr = abi.simpleEncode(
    "invest(uint)","0xc").toString("hex")
console.log (newstr)
```

What you did was play a hand in generating a binary interface for the method *"invest(stock id)"*. The resulting hex value appears in single quotes. Apt is the time to invoke the ***invest*** operation.

```
# seth contract call alias
46f7c50dd835ca3538c8e0302f9b3faf385f708d
2afcf48000000000000000000000000000000000000000000000000
00000000000000013 --wait
```

The syntax for the seth contract call is [alias] [address] [data or operation]. The address starting with '46f7..' results from the contract being pushed into Sawtooth. This is different from the address that came about initially when the account took birth. When you run this, you should see a result somewhat resembling the output below.

```
Contract called
Transaction Receipt: {"TransactionID":
"af39801b662fc85885db271399bf414433cbb642476b6dac779d46
3c94a70b7a74b3c036454e6048ca6252739bcd5d5fcd7106915ba
10553421a40b67e59a258",
 "GasUsed": 114, "ReturnValue":
"0000000000000000000000000000000000000000000000000000000001"
}
```

 As we go back to the discussions on financial planning which we had set aside to experiment with Hyperledger, we realize that in the current challenging economic climate, it's never too early to save for the rainy day.

The Financial Planning and Advisory system through stochastic learning can become an expert in wealth management, financial planning, investment management, and retirement planning. Laying out the goals for retirement and visualizing for the client, a successful, secure retirement scheme can be its key supporting function. The system can use the information to model and analyze specific situations simulating various scenarios. From the analysis, the advisory can offer practical, independent advice that can nail down the retirement goals.

The system must query on the risks the client thinks he or she may face, including longevity, market volatility and inflation and use them as constraints in the model. It can provision for sustainable withdrawal rates in the plan. The system identifies which assets to draw from first, whether they are taxable, tax-deferred or tax-free accounts.

Education is another large expense; current trends suggest that the price tag for a college degree will only continue to increase. Saving enough money for college is yet another tough investment the client faces. The system can suggest ways to save for a child's education. Every suggestion can become a timeline in the blockchain database. Copies of the blockchain database are automatically replicated to different nodes - attorneys and others become a party to the transactions.

The planning system comprising the distributed ledger system offers an independent, practical advice to help the client structure, implement, finance and manage such critical savings. If the client has considered leaving financial legacy for the family and future generations, then estate planning – the accumulation, management, conservation and transfer of assets – is a critical component of comprehensive wealth management strategy. The system can work with the client to develop an estate plan customized for a client's specific situation and ensure the client's wishes are carried out.

Estate planning process includes reassessing how the client wants the assets distributed upon death and how they continue to be managed if the client were incapacitated. Such planning would include calculating the foreseeable estate taxes, reducing tax liability and recommend on practical strategies to increase the value of assets for future generations. Planning for the days ahead to protect the client family during a health crisis or other adversities is another critical savings plan. Getting older is a fact of life, but often one does not plan for it. Having provisions in the application to arrive at an independent, practical elderly care keeps the family prepared and protected. In empowering one's independence, the smart contract provisions for the client to take control of one's life again should the marriage end in a divorce.

Every client has constraints, where timeframe, liquidity and risk tolerance determine the constraints. Timeframe is perhaps the most important one among them. A blockchain-ed system is able to guarantee the integrity of the data, spanning decades. Many such factors were carefully introduced into the composer Smart Contract we just ran.

Crucial goal of short-time investing may require a low risk portfolio differing significantly from a longer-term goal. Liquidity is another important factor; when amount converted to cash without significant loss can sometimes re-balance the portfolio. Most people want to achieve multiple financial objectives. "If clients have a young child, their retirement goals may be quite different and then may want to buy a lake house in the not-too-distant future. We must help them designate funds for each of these," Gartman says. He recommends maintaining a diversified portfolio to work toward financial goals while also mitigating risk. "Spread the clients' assets across investment vehicles," he says. "The purpose is to create a balance so all assets are not in any one category."

As a Financial Planner,	
I would like to carry out my client's goals, expectations and constraints. I'd consider it a success if the investments he or she makes has a positive impact on the person. I wish to make the client aware of the risks of any asset allocation. Setting a planned portfolio to an active or deactivated state must be easy. I should be able to deal with the client, or a trust or a power of attorney. All transactions must occur in a strictly secure and permissioned manner.	
Expected outcome:	A successful portfolio that I can re-visit now and then.
Failed outcome:	A portfolio that fails to meet the goals and expectations.

Design

Summarizing the discussion up till now, a comprehensive Smart Contract evolves that addresses several of the concerns expressed in the requirements.

```
/**
 * Wealth Management - Financial Advisory.
 * License - Apache 2.0
 */
pragma solidity ^0.4.17;

contract FinancialPlan {
    /** all parties are known by their key pair */
    address public individual;
    address public party;
    address public trust;
    address public powerOfAttorney;
    enum PortfolioStatus {ACTIVE,DEACTIVATED,MERGED}
    PortfolioStatus public status = PortfolioStatus.ACTIVE;
    event ChangePortfolioValue (address
        portfolio, uint oldValue, uint newValue);
    /**
     * Allocation definition: the distribution of investment
     * across money market, bonds and stock
     */
    enum AllocType {COIN, MONEYMARKET,
        BONDS, STOCK, INSURANCE, REALESTATE}
```

```
struct Allocation {
    AllocType allocType;
    uint percent;
}


/**
* Rainy Day or hidden goals are not explicit goals,
* they are more contingency - like an auto accident.
* Intermediate are those with finite time objectives
* like college education, wedding
* lifetime goals are meant for retirement
*/


struct Goals {
    address clientId;
    Allocation rainyDay;
    Allocation intermediate;
    Allocation lifetime;
    uint basicLivingExpenses;
    uint fixedTerminalExpenses;
    uint inflatableExpenses;
}


/**
* Constraints are client's aversion to risk
* Keeping percent of investments in cash is a customer's safe bet
*/


struct Constraints {
    address clientId;
    uint liquidity;
    uint marketability;
    uint threshold;
}
```

```
/**
* Expectations from an investment what the cash flows
* are from different types
*/
  struct Expectations {
    address clientId;
    uint cashFlowBonds;
    uint cashFlowStock;
    uint cashReserve;
  }


/**
* Both market and cash flow projections also look into anticipated inflation
* and forecast portfolio value
*/

  struct Projections {
    address clientId;
    uint anticipatedCashFlow;
    uint anticipatedInflation;
    uint anticipatedPortfolioValue;
    uint chanceSuccess;
  }


/**
* Client or customer defined by an id. Could be a party also
* governmentID such as SSN. Maybe redundant
*/

  struct Client {
    address clientId;
    bytes32 governmentId;
    bytes2 nationality;
  }

  enum AssetType {ASSET, LIABILITY}
```

```
struct Investment {
    address assetId;
    string assetGroup;
    string assetClass;
    string assetSummary;
    string taxJurisdiction;
    bytes10 currency;
    AssetType assetType;
    uint value;
    uint projectedValue;
    uint interest;
    uint dividends;
    uint capitalGains;
}

// Part of retirement and Estate Planning
struct Estate {
    string assetId;
    string distributionUponDeath;
    uint value;
    uint estateTaxes;
    uint probateFees;
    string directionsForDisburtion;
}
enum RecurringBasis {DAILY, WEEKLY,
MONTHLY, QUARTERLY, ANNUAL, ONETIMEONLY}
struct Care {
    bytes8 careId;
    string referenceNum;
    string description;
    uint cost;
    RecurringBasis basis;
    uint monthlyPremium;
    uint256 expirationDate;
}
```

```
struct Insurance {
    bytes8 insuranceId;
    string referenceNum;
    string description;
    string insuranceType;
    uint value;
    RecurringBasis basis;
    uint premium;
    uint256 expirationDate;
}
struct DivorcePlan {
    bytes8 divorcePlanId;
    string referenceNum;
    string description;
    uint256 expirationDate;
}

struct AssetPortfolio {
    bytes32 portfolioId;
    Investment[] investments;
    address[] clients;
    Estate[] estates;
    bool reviewed;
    Goals goals;
    Constraints constraints;
    Expectations expectations;
    Projections projections;
    string[] disclosures;
    Care[] care;
    Insurance[] insurances;
    DivorcePlan[] divorcePlans;
}

enum AccountStatus {ACTIVE, INACTIVE, DORMANT}
AssetPortfolio[] assetPortfolios;
```

```
struct FCAccount {
    address accountId;
    AccountStatus status;
    address client;
    AssetPortfolio[] assetPortfolio;
    string[] notes;
    uint256 beginningDate;
}

function getPortfolios() internal returns (AssetPortfolio[]) {
    return assetPortfolios;
}

function onModifyPortfolio(bytes32 portfolioId, Investment inv)
        public returns (bool) {
    var invid = inv.assetId;
    var invest = inv;
    var result = false;
    for (uint i = 0; i < assetPortfolios.length; i++) {
        if (assetPortfolios[i].portfolioId == portfolioId) {
            for (uint j = 0;j<assetPortfolios[i].investments.length; j++) {
                if (assetPortfolios[i].investments[j].assetId==invid) {
                    assetPortfolios[i].investments[j] = invest;
                    result = true;
                }
            }
        }
    }
    return result;
}
}
```

As explained before, you could use either Truffle, Seth CLI or a custom app in Python or Node-JS to deploy the contract. The contract in our case is relatively large and the 'gas' consumed may be significant.

I have had my share of success and failures in deploying them to the container. There is always room for reducing the contract to smaller chunks. Knitting the pieces into one contract achieves the purpose of this book.

Node.JS Express allows route handling and middleware supervision of RESTful invocations. With Sawtooth-Seth and Fabric running as services, we introduce a separate middleware server that manages the functions and optimizations for the financial planning application but also provides posts to the RPC server running on Sawtooth.

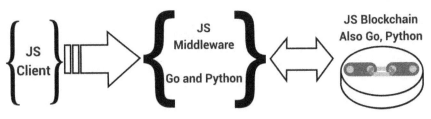

Figure 11 - Technology Stack

The middleware runs through callbacks that sit on top of the actual request handlers as shown in Figure 11. It takes the same parameters to re-route the request. Much like a delegate. To upload the smart contract written in Solidity, a client written for Seth-RPC in Node.JS can serve the purpose.

```
/*sethrpclib.js*/
/*jshint esversion: 6 */
let request = require('request');
```

The service at *"seth-rpc"* accepts JSON-RPC posts only. Though used are parameters such as gas and gas price, Sawtooth does not care about them, they are targeted for other Ethereum networks.

```
function postSethRPC() {
request({url: 'http://localhost:3030',
    method: 'POST',json: {"jsonrpc": "2.0",
    "id": 19,
    "method": "eth_sendTransaction", "
    params": [{"from":
      "0x659f1526b3a62a81039ab840d71eac5751370b36",
      "gas": "0x6691b7",
    "gasPrice": "0x174876e800",
    "data":
"0x60606040523415600e57600080fd5b609a8061001c6000396000f3006060604
05260043610603e5763ffffffff7c0100000000000000000000000000000000000000
0000000000000000006000350417663c6888fa181146043575b600080fd5b3415
604d57600080fd5b60566004356068565b60405190815260200160405180910039
0f35b600702905600a165627a7a723058206f4a604d7fb9f559014a48b1e2be9ab
50644a5984e8bbb1b6496425aa59f1ee00029"
    }]}
}, function(error, response, body){
    console.log('Seth RPC Response', body);
})};
```

You can test the instance of this code by running sethrpclib.js on Node.JS or by exposing the library for other clients to use.

```
postSethRPC();
module.exports = postSethRPC;
```

For the node client to run, the *'request'* library is needed. Besides, if the computer operating system fails to support the new Docker and you are using the older *Docker Toolbox*, then run the *Docker Quickstart Terminal* and carry out the commands in the preconfigured terminal.

Ensure you make a note of the Docker IP address which appears when the shell starts. In the JavaScript code, the URL will change to url: 'http://192.168.99.100:3030'

```
$ npm install request
```

The code body is a single function *'postSethRPC'* that requires two important parameters – the 'from' address or the address of the account and the application binary code of the solidity compiled code. To compile the *Portfolio.sol* created earlier, run the following command.

```
$ solcjs Portfolio.sol --binary
$ cat Portfolio_sol_Portfolio.bin
```

You must copy the code as it appears in hex to the place in the code shown as data to run this Node-JS application. The code is ready to be run now. In fact, you can spend some time to complete the rest of the middleware code that listens to the requests coming from an HTML or PHP client. If the post requires the data to be transmitted to Sawtooth-Seth, the method *postSeth* will route it to the URL.

```
/*jshint esversion: 6 */
```

```
let express = require('express');
let app = express();
let router = express.Router();
let postSethRPC = require('./sethrpclib');
// seth rpc client logger
let sethclientLogger = function(req, res, next){
  console.log('Log Request: ', req);
  console.log('Log Response: ', res);
  next();
}
// No mount path on this middleware operation
// This code is executed for every request to the router
router.use(function (req, res, next) {
  console.log('Start Time:', Date.now());
  next();
})
```

The help.html though declared in the 'public' folder, has no listing in this book. It is a standard static html and I leave it to the reader to design and develop it.

```
// handler for help path, which renders a special page
router.get('/help', function (req, res, next) {
    res.render('help.html');
    next();
})
```

When the "*postseth*" operation is invoked through the command http://localhost:9999/postseth, the corresponding "*postSethRPC*" exported by the previous *sethrpclib.js* file is called upon.

```
// Post function that calls Seth RPC
```

```
router.post('/postseth', postSethRPC);
// POST method route
router.post('/postsethrpc', function (req, res, next) {
    postSethRPC();
    res.send('POST request to the homepage');
    next();
})
// mount the router on the app
var options = {
    dotfiles: 'ignore', etag: false,
    extensions: ['htm', 'html'],
    index: false, redirect: false,
    setHeaders: function (res, path, stat) {
      res.set('x-timestamp', Date.now());
    }
}
app.use(express.static('public', options));
app.use('/', router);
app.use(sethclientLogger);
console.log('Seth RPC Client Listening at port 9999');
app.listen(9999);
```

The middleware running on Node-JS 'express' provides the necessary isolation and cushion to the back-end database or blockchain.

```
$ npm install express
```

You are free to add third party loggers and enhance the source code. I have kept the code simple to manage. The above application also uses a 'public' folder where static html files can reside. As you must have noticed, the Node-JS application runs on the port 9999 and listens for requests and events. On receiving a http POST, it redirects to the *postSethRPC* function defined in the *'sethrpclib.js'* file.

Once you fire-up the middleware, you can use Postman[22] or 'curl' to post the data to the middleware (POST:localhost:999/postsethrpc).

```
$ node sethrpcrun.js
```

As with Node-JS, you can also create a client with Python 3.6.x and "post" into Sawtooth-seth instance. For the python code to run, you will need to install 'Urllib' and JSON libraries additionally.

```python
import urllib.request
import json

sethjson = {"jsonrpc": "2.0", "id": 19,
    "method": "eth_sendTransaction",
    "params": [
    {"from":
        "0x659f1526b3a62a81039ab840d71eac5751370b36",
        "gas": "0x6691b7",
    "gasPrice": "0x174876e800",
    "data":
"0x60606040523415600e57600080fd5b609a8061001c6000396000f3006060604
05260043610603e5763ffffffff7c01000000000000000000000000000000000000000
00000000000000000000600035041663c6888fa181146043575b600080fd5b3415
604d57600080fd5b60566004356068565b604051908152602001604051809103910
0f35b600702905600a165627a7a723058206f4a604d7fb9f559014a48b1e2be9ab
50644a5984e8bbb1b6496425aa59f1ee00029" }]}
url = http://192.168.99.100:3030
```

22

https://chrome.google.com/webstore/detail/postman/fhbjgbiflinjbdggehcddcb
ncdddomop?hl=en

```
# create the request
request = urllib.request.Request(url)
# add appropriate header
request.add_header('Content-Type', 'application/json; charset=utf-8')
```

The 'json.dumps' method is a JSON encoder. The command serializes the object produced. Remember, JSON is not intrinsic to Python but JavaScript and therefore needs the libraries to achieve the serialization. If the application finds out the object is not serializable, then the instruction fails.

```
jsonSentData = json.dumps(sethjson)
jsonSentAsBytes = jsonSentData.encode('utf-8')
                # changed to bytes
request.add_header('Content-Length', len(jsonSentAsBytes))
print (jsonSentAsBytes)
response = urllib.request.urlopen(request, jsonSentAsBytes)
```

The Python code's behavior is analogous to the Node-JS SethRPCLib.js file and provides the ability to 'post' the Smart Contract to an account in Sawtooth Blockchain. Back to where we had left, the client's risk appetite can rise and fall along the investment timeline, which measures both age and how much time is spent before achieving any financial goal. For example, as the client nears retirement, the risk tolerance decreases because there is less time to recover any money lost from market fluctuations, Gartman says. But when the client is planning for retirement 30 or 40 years out, there is always the appetite to tolerate a higher level of investment risk.

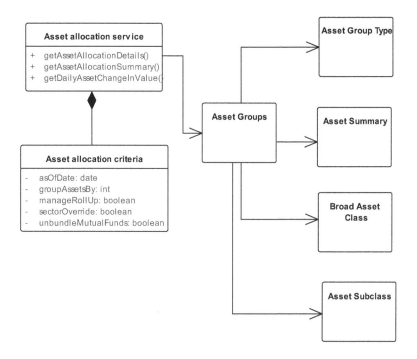

Figure 12 - Asset Allocation Service

 For the different phases and processes, several services, contracts can fulfill the needs of the processes to meet their goals. Illustrated are examples of such services. Starting with asset allocation service having a few API methods. The Asset allocation service provides methods to extract the asset allocation details and summary. The portfolio assets return as sets of groups, with predetermined group types, broad asset class types and sub classes of assets. For a moment, lets pause and write a simplified contract for asset allocation on Sawtooth-Seth. I will let the reader try his or her hand at creating a similar contract for Hyperledger Composer.

Solidity

```
pragma solidity ^0.4.17;

contract AssetAlloc {
  address asset;
  function allocDetail(uint date,
    string stock) public returns (address) {
    return asset;
  }
  function allocSumm(uint date, string stock)
    public returns (address) {
    return asset;
  }
}
```

The contract is an oversimplified asset allocation, compared to the class diagram. Operations in the asset allocation service take five parameters as criteria in the original class model, which has been downgraded in the example to keep the code readable. The idea is to build a simple middleware to connect to the Hyperledger Sawtooth-Seth system. I hope you have installed the Solidity compiler by now, if not here is the NPM command again.

```
$ solcjs AssetAlloc.sol –bin
```

You can run the compiler within the *seth-rpc* container, unlock the 'alias' account and introduce the asset allocation contract.

```
$ seth contract create --wait alias
6060604052341561000f57600080fd5b6102218061001e6063ed7
9f511146100f7575b60 ...
```

Next, we will write a Node-JS Express middleware that can invoke the contract functions and offer its services to the external world. Here I will offer choices of both Node-JS Express and Python. Fabric and Sawtooth-Seth actively support both programming languages. The design of the middleware application uses a 'bootstrapped' server that can accept incoming http (REST) requests and route the requests to different end points. Express in Node-JS offers an elegant routing engine. A function *postAASethRPC* that can post to asset allocation accessible through Seth-RPC accepts the divided data as input.

The data directed to this function uses the Ethereum ABI *(application binary interface)* library to generate the code in hexadecimal. An application binary interface (ABI) is an accepted interface between two program modules; often, one of these modules is a library or operating system facility, and the other is a program that is being run by a user[23].

```
/*jshint esversion: 6 */

let express = require('express');
let request = require('request');
let abi = require('ethereumjs-abi');
let web3 = require('web3');

let app = express();
let router = express.Router();
```

---

[23] https://en.wikipedia.org/wiki/Application_binary_interface

```
// No mount path on this middleware operation
// This code is executed for every request to the router
router.use(function (req, res, next) {
  console.log('Start Time:', Date.now());
  next();
})
```

The Asset Allocation POST command entails two key parameters – the address of the alias or the account that has been unlocked before, where the compiled Solidity code has been uploaded. Such a function also needs to delegate the call to the '*allocDetail*' function in the contract.

```
function postAASethRPC(allocData) {
  request({
    url: 'http://127.0.0.1:3030',
    method: 'POST',
    json: {"jsonrpc": "2.0", "id": 19,
      "method": "eth_sendTransaction",

      "params": [
      {"from":
        "0x345ca3e014aaf5dca488057592ee47305d9b3e10",
        "gas": "0x6691b7",
        "gasPrice": "0x174876e800",
        "data": allocData
    }]}
  }, function(error, response, body){
    console.log('Seth RPC Response', body);
})};
```

That comprises the middleware sub-stack to handle the asset-allocation requests. It provides the API to the internal method *allocDetail* in sending the ABI hex of the method call to run in the Sawtooth-Seth environment. Along with the invocation, it also results in the transaction being stored in a block in the underlying blockchain.

```
router.get('/assetAllocationDetails/:asOfDate/:groupAssetsBy',
function (req, res, next) {
    console.log(req.params.asOfDate +
                            req.params.groupAssetsBy);
    let strtoseth = abi.simpleEncode("allocDetail(uint,uint)",
        req.params.asOfDate,
        req.params.groupAssetsBy).toString("hex")
    postAASethRPC(strtoseth);
    res.send(strtoseth);
})


// handler for asset allocation summary service
router.get('/assetAllocationSummary/:asOfDate/:groupAssetsBy',
  function (req, res, next) {
  console.log(req.params.asOfDate);
  let strtoseth = abi.simpleEncode("allocSumm(uint,uint)",
      req.params.asOfDate,
      req.params.groupAssetsBy).toString("hex")
  postAASethRPC(strtoseth);
  res.send(strtoseth);
})
app.use('/', router);
console.log('Asset Allocation Service Listening at port 9999');
app.listen(9999);
```

One may use the browser to invoke the allocation service through the middle-tier. If you start the Node-JS application within the Docker container, then it may require a few extra tweaks to access the end-points.

http://localhost:9999/assetAllocationDetails/0/stocks

Another such essential financial planning service is the cash flow service.

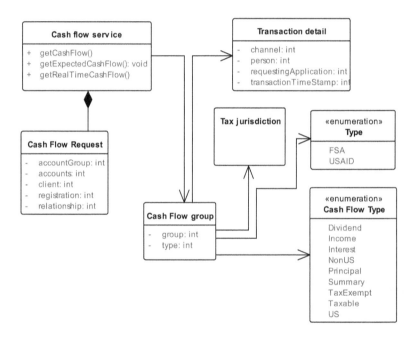

Figure 13 – Cash flow Service

The cash flow is one more single-responsibility micro-service needed to monitor the portfolio. Some elements may be commonly shared with the asset allocation service through service-to-service invocations. The service includes information on all transactions that are conducted for log and audit purpose.

 The JavaScript code is just a skeleton code that lays out the micro-service bare bones. Three operations as indicated in the class model in Figure 13 are defined as 'GET' requests in the JavaScript web-service.

```
let express = require('express')
let app = express()
let router = express.Router()

var myLogger = function (req, res, next) {
   console.log('LOGGED')
   next()
}
router.use(function (req, res, next) {
   console.log('Time:', Date.now())
   next()
})
router.get('/actual/:client',
function (req, res, next) {
   console.log('Request URL:', req.originalUrl)
   console.log(req.params.client)
   res.send({ 'Got it':
     'Actual Cashflow summary on its way'})
})
router.get('/expected/:client',
function (req, res, next) {
   console.log('Request URL:', req.originalUrl)
   console.log(req.params.client)
   res.send({ 'Got it':
     'Expected Cashflow summary on its way'})
})
```

```
router.get('/realtime/:client',
function (req, res, next) {
    console.log('Request URL:', req.originalUrl)
    console.log(req.params.client)
    res.send({'Got it':
        'Real-time Cashflow summary on its way'})
})

app.use('/cashflow/', router)

app.use(myLogger)
console.log('Cashflow Listening at port 9991')

app.listen(9991)
```

A typical invocation to this service and calling out the method 'realtime' would resemble:

http://localhost:9991/cashflow/realtime/cid001

Next in the financial planning comes the gain and loss service, which tells the client how the portfolio is doing. It is a service that works within the constraints of a fiscal year and other, different groups.

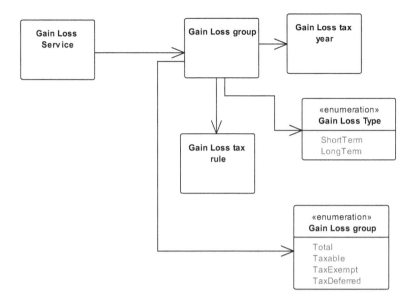

Figure 14 - Gain and Loss service

Illustrated next is the Balance Sheet service in figure 14.

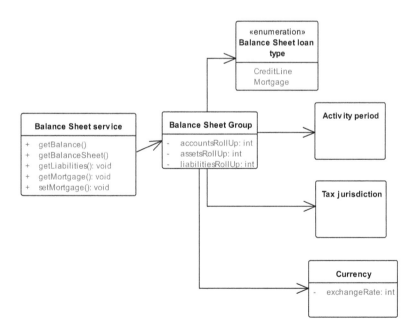

Figure 15 - Balance Sheet service

Balancesheet JavaScript service running on Node-JS is also a skeletal micro-service. The reader is free to expand and complete the functionality.

```
let express = require('express')
let app = express()
let router = express.Router()

var myLogger = function (req, res, next) {
   console.log('LOGGED')
   next()
}
router.use(function (req, res, next) {
   console.log('Time:', Date.now());
      next();
})
router.get('/actual/:client',
function (req, res, next) {
   console.log('Request URL:', req.originalUrl)
   console.log(req.params.client)
   res.send({ 'Got it':
     'Actual balance sheet summary on its way' })
})

router.get('/balance/:client',
function (req, res, next) {
   console.log('Request URL:', req.originalUrl)
   console.log(req.params.client)
   res.send({ 'Got it': 'Balance sheet
          (balance) summary on its way' })
})
```

```
router.get('/liabilities/:client',
function (req, res, next) {
    console.log('Request URL:', req.originalUrl)
    console.log(req.params.client)
    res.send({'Got it': 'Balance sheet
            (liabilities) summary on its way'})
})

app.use('/balancesheet/', router)
app.use(myLogger)
console.log('Balancesheet Listening
            at port 9992')
app.listen(9992)
```

You may use this service from a client or browser, or the 'Postman' client.

http://localhost:9992/balancesheet/actual/cid001

The financial-account service appears last. Such a service though named 'account', differs from the 'account' created in blockchains. You'd reckon the preferred name to be 'financial-account'.

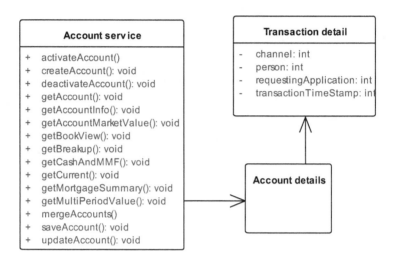

Figure 16 - Account service

User story	
As a Financial Planner,	
I would like to setup a financial account for my client after necessary verification and obtaining the client's approval on the agreement and fees. The financial account belongs to a designated owner, but other persons can be attached to the account such as household, trust, attorney and others. Personal identities are kept secure through hashed certificates as identity.	
Expected outcome:	A secure financial account for the client.
Failed outcome:	An account that fails to meet security conditions.

This is the proposed overall architecture for all the services. As the reader, you are free to modify the architecture and tweak it to a financial-institution's in-house architecture or a cloud mandated one; it is a good practice to maintain architectural consistency throughout and ensure the principles are consistent with actual implementations. For the Account Service, I have defined a contract that is compliant to Hyperledger Composer and Fabric. This gives the reader a perspective of both Sawtooth and Fabric.

 In defining the contract, or the model within the business network, the syntax and semantics conform to the Composer. Hyperledger Composer comes with an elegant REST server and a useful REST client. JSON requests designed later in the chapter can be run through this REST client.

Composer

```
namespace com.devb.financialplanning


asset FinancialAccount identified by accountId {
  o String    accountId
  --> Person   person
  o String    requestingApplication
}
```

```
participant Person identified by personId {
  o String personId
  o String firstName
  o String lastName
}

transaction SaveAccount {
  --> Person person
  --> FinancialAccount financialAccount
}
```

The logic.js is where the transaction logic gets defined in JavaScript. You will notice the important use of callbacks through 'async' and 'await'. In a decentralized data management scenario, transactions have to wait for a consensus before they are written to the blockchain. The logic also uses the 'promise' notion when committing transactions.

```
'use strict';
/**
 * Process a property that is held for sale
 * @param{com.devb.financialplanning.SaveAccount}acc
 * @transaction
 */
async function onSave(acc) {
    console.log('### Setting account '
    + financialAccount.toString());
    const registry = await
       getAssetRegistry(
       'com.devb.financialplanning.FinancialAccount');
    await registry.update(financialAccount);
}
```

The access control list as before, provides fine grained control within the network.

```
rule Default {
    description: "Allow participants access to resources"
    participant: "ANY"
    operation: ALL
    resource: "com.devb.financialplanning.*"
    action: ALLOW
}

rule SystemACL {
    description:  "System permitted all access"
    participant: "org.hyperledger.composer.system.Participant"
    operation: ALL
    resource: "org.hyperledger.composer.system.**"
    action: ALLOW
}

rule NetworkAdminUser {
    description: "Grant BN admins full access"
    participant: "org.hyperledger.composer.system.NetworkAdmin"
    operation: ALL
    resource: "**"
    action: ALLOW
}

rule NetworkAdminSystem {
    description: "Grant BN admins full access to system"
    participant: "org.hyperledger.composer.system.NetworkAdmin"
    operation: ALL
    resource: "org.hyperledger.composer.system.**"
    action: ALLOW
}
```

The JSON for defining the person and the account is illustrated below. Hyperledger REST client manages to run the two requests. If you have other tools like Postman, you can also use it to run the requests.

```
{
    "$class": "com.devb.financialplanning.Person",
    "personId": "1",
    "firstName": "Joe",
    "lastName": "Doe"
}
```

```
{
    "$class": "com.devb.financialplanning.FinancialAccount",
    "accountId": "2",
    "person": "resource:com.devb.financialplanning.Person#1",
    "requestingApplication": "1234"
}
```

And the transaction for saving the account would be.

```
{"$class": "com.devb.financialplanning.SaveAccount",
    "person": "resource:com.devb.financialplanning.Person#1",
    "financialAccount":
      "resource:com.devb.financialplanning.FinancialAccount#2"
}
```

Since there is much more to financial planning, I will cover the remaining chapter with just models and description, because representing everything through a middleware server may just get too intimidating.

Fear of risk tends to restrict the customer's investment. One of the key features of a wealth management system would be in assisting clients in grappling the frightening specter of risk. Benjamin Graham once stated "Investment decisions are 25 percent intelligence and 75 percent psychology." Clients have difficulty estimating the risks of future events just the same way we have in predicting weather. Without an exact science, the psychology takes over common sense. Either knowledge, rationality, values or emotions determine the decisions and the outcome.

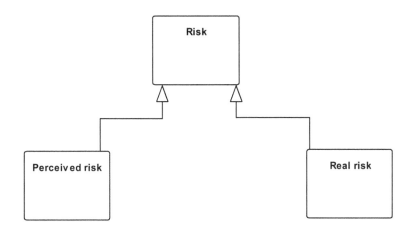

Figure 17 - Real and perceived risk

 Predicting the future from the past, often dictates the client's mental makeup. Experiences from the past, whether successful or failed are often superficial and may be significant only in the short term, but anything long term is different. Sometimes investors decide on social impulse and forestall logical actions to avoid appearing foolish. To avoid the pain, they basically do nothing. Another such dilemma comes from not being able to distinguish between perceived and real risk. Besides, there is always the confusion between tax reduction versus after-tax maximization. Perceived risk sometimes results in paying excess taxes, the real risk comes from not maximizing the after-tax returns. The advisory comes with questions and suggestions to mitigate such feelings. This subject on risk tolerance through financial products can be a whole book by itself[24].

---

[24] Harold Evensky – Wealth Management

Questions and scoring service can return a risk score. One can categorize the person from such a score and through machine learning and verbalization, the perceived risk can be downplayed, and the client rewarded with a better portfolio.

Strategy for data gathering and analysis

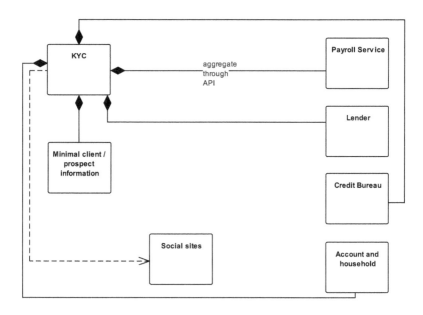

Figure 18 - Data gathering strategy

Asset allocation service analyzes an investor's portfolio to determine the portfolio's asset allocation and asset class assignments of each holding in the portfolio. The service returns the analysis at the portfolio level with an allocation for each asset allocation sub-class, depending on the chosen model. Shown is the asset allocation service below.

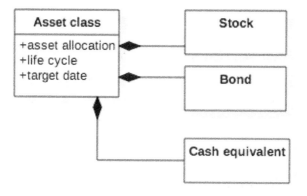

Figure 19 - Asset classes

The portfolio manager decides on the distribution of asset classes. The portfolio has many advantages.

- A complete picture of the investor's financial life
- The health of the portfolio
- Future planning

Establishing an appropriate asset mix is a dynamic process, and it plays a key role in determining the portfolio's overall risk and return. Client's portfolio asset mix should reflect the goals at any point in time. Here we outline some different strategies of establishing asset allocations; we examine their basic management approaches.

Different Asset Allocation types

The first method establishes and adheres to a 'base policy mix' - a proportional combination of assets based on expected rates of return for each asset class. For example, if stocks have historically returned 10% per year and bonds have returned 5% per year, a mix of 50% stocks and 50% bonds would be expected to return 7.5% per year[25].

---

[25] Harold Evensky's Wealth Management

The second allocation type, unlike the first, strategic asset allocation which suggests a buy-and-hold strategy, even as the shift in asset values cause a drift from the initially established policy mix. To avoid such, the client may adopt a constant-weighting asset allocation. This approach continually re-balances the portfolio. There are no hard-and-fast rules for timing the portfolio in re-balancing itself under strategic or constant-weighting asset allocation. However, a common rule of thumb is that the portfolio gets re-balanced to its original mix when any asset class in the portfolio deviates beyond 5% from its original value. Over the long run, a strategic asset allocation strategy may seem relatively rigid. The client may occasionally engage in short-term, tactical deviations from the mix to capitalize on unusual or exceptional investment opportunities. This flexibility adds a 'market timing' component to the portfolio, allowing you to participate in economic conditions more favorable to one asset class over others[26].

An asset allocation fund is a mutual fund that provides investors with a portfolio of a fixed or variable mix of the three main asset classes - stocks, bonds and cash equivalents - in a variety of securities. Some asset allocation funds maintain a specific proportion of asset classes over time, while others vary the proportional composition in response to changes in the economy and investment markets.[27] Asset allocation mutual funds come in several varieties.

---

[26] 6 Asset Allocation Strategies That Work | Investopedia
http://www.investopedia.com/articles/04/031704.asp#ixzz4WXUXvCvN
[27] Asset Allocation Fund Definition | Investopedia
http://www.investopedia.com/terms/a/aaf.asp#ixzz4UvPJNjwF

Largely, "balanced fund" implies a fixed-mix of stocks and bonds, such as 60% stocks and 40% bonds. "Life-cycle" or "target-date" funds used in retirement plans, usually have a mix of stocks, bonds and cash equivalent securities that starts out with a higher risk-return position and gradually turns less risky as the investor nears retirement. So-called "life-style," or actively managed asset-allocation funds provide the active management of a fund's asset classes in response to market conditions.

Several collections on asset allocation types have come through research papers. *PortfolioAllocation*[28] is one such JavaScript library[29] to allocate portfolios of financial assets - to compute the proportions of a given set of financial instruments such as stocks, bonds, exchange traded funds - ETFs, mutual funds and others to hold in a portfolio in order to optimize specific quantitative criteria related to this portfolio. Here is an example portfolio allocation using the library where all numbers are randomly generated. Instead of a random list of asset classes, you may enter real asset classes, their worth and potentially fill the portfolio with real world samples.

User story
As a Portfolio Holder,
I would like to run simulations on likely investments and compare different asset allocation results. I would like to preview the allocation percentages and walk through different 'what if' scenarios.

---

[28] https://www.npmjs.com/package/portfolio-allocation
[29] https://github.com/lequant40/portfolio_allocation_js

Expected outcome:	A trial portfolio, I can monitor.
Failed outcome:	An incorrect portfolio that can be misleading.

 We turn the requirements into a JavaScript code that can use statistical ways to allocate asset classes.

```
/* eslint-disable */
/* jshint esversion:6 */

let pa = require('portfolio-allocation');
```

AssetAllocation is the class defined in JavaScript with the method "doWeightedRisk". The method contains different scenarios wherein equal weights, equal risks are called from the library and computed against.

```
let AssetAllocation = class {
   constructor (portfolioSize, portfolioType) {
      this.portfolioSize = portfolioSize;
      this.portfolioType = portfolioType;
   }
   // Assets allocation module
   doWeightedRisk() {
```

```
// Rounded weights portfolio
console.log('Rounded Weights');
// Example with static data
let testValues = [
    [0.7373, 0.2627, 0], [0.5759, 0.0671, 0.3570],
    [0.22, 0.66, 0.12], [0.22, 0.66, 0.12], [0.5, 0.49, 0.01]
];
let testGridIndices = [10, 10, 1, 5, 1];
let reslt;
let i = 0;
console.log('Examples of rounding.')
console.log('Use rounded wts with AA')
for (i = 0;i < testValues.length; ++i) {
    reslt = pa.roundedWeights(testValues[i],
            testGridIndices[i]);
    console.log(reslt);
}
// Covariance matrix
let sigma = [
    [0.0100, 0.0090, 0.0010], [0.0090, 0.0100, 0.0010],
    [0.0010, 0.0010, 0.0100]
];
// Compute MDP weights
let wts = pa.mostDiversifiedWeights(sigma,
        {eps: 1e-10, maxIter: 10000});
console.log('Example of most diversified weights.')
console.log(wts);
console.log('Example Equal Weights');
// Generate a number of assets
let pList = Math.floor(Math.random() *
        (this.portfolioSize - 1 + 1) + 1);
// Compute Equal Weights
wts = pa.equalWeights(pList);
console.log('Equal weights for portfolio size '+pList)
console.log(wts);
console.log('Example Equal Risk');
```

```
    // use the same list and generate n random variances
    let sigma1 = new Array(pList);
    for (let i = 0; i < pList; ++i) {
        sigma1[i] = 1 - Math.random();
    }
    // Compute ERB weights
    wts = pa.equalRiskBudgetWeights(sigma1);
    // Check the number of output weights
    console.log('Portfolio size '+wts.length);
    console.log(wts);
    // ERC portfolio
    wts = pa.equalRiskContributionWeights(
            [[0.1, 0, 0], [0, 0.2, 0],[0, 0, 0.3]]);
    console.log('Equal risk contribution ');
    console.log(wts);
  }
}
// program starts here
console.log("** Program start **");
let aa = new AssetAllocation(18, "equalWeights");
aa.doWeightedRisk();
console.log("** Program end **");
// program ends here
```

 The relative percentages of core asset classes such as equities, fixed income and cash, along with real estate and international holdings have their place in a mutual fund, exchange-traded fund-based portfolio. Asset classes are broken further into growth stocks, value stocks, market capitalizations ranging from small, medium to large; and various types of fixed income such as government bonds, corporate bonds and municipal bonds.

Asset class breakdown is a simple way to determine the approximate risk profile of a fund. Exposure to higher equities yields a higher return, but with greater risk than a portfolio made of high percentage of bonds. Many analysts and economists feel that proper asset allocation is the biggest determinant of overall returns - far greater than sector selection or individual security selection. A typical micro-service must provide access to a summary of allocation of all accounts. Closely linked to other atomic services like advisory, portfolio, customer and account, the asset allocation is a nimble micro-service defined herein.

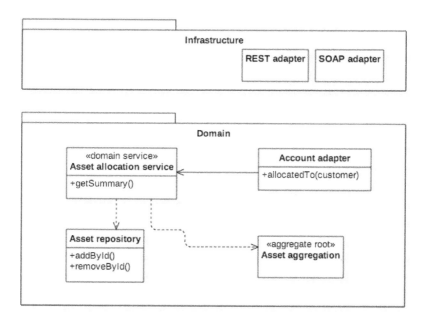

Figure 20 - Asset allocation micro-service

Cash flow management

Cash flow service tracks and evaluates the income and expenses, a clear management of the P&L part of the portfolio.

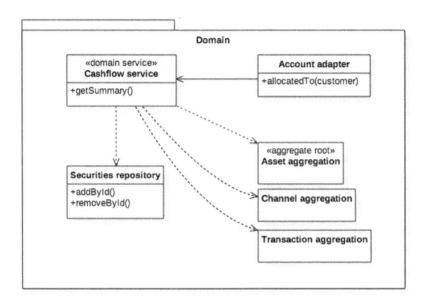

Figure 21 - Cashflow Service

Gain-Loss Service

Besides offering a comprehensive performance of the assets, gain-loss service also takes part in tax preparation and management.

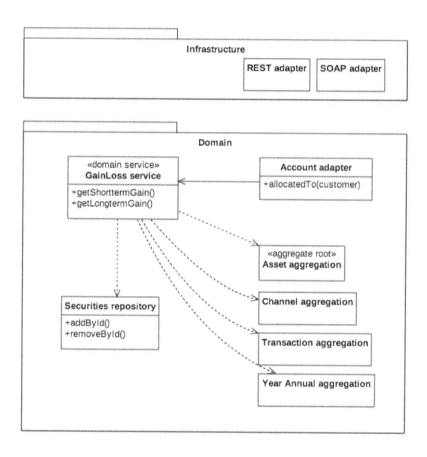

Figure 22 - Gain-Loss service

Balance Sheet Service

Balance sheets are a key business financial report that help to analyze trends in the assets.

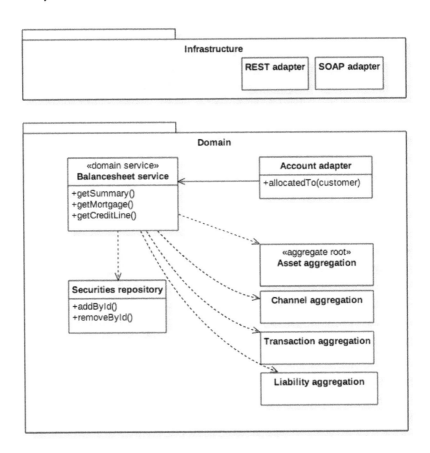

Figure 23 - Balance Sheet Service

To manage investments in stock, bonds and funds, details of the **Order Management Services** take precedence.

Trade order states

A 'trade' flows through several tasks, changes its state from portfolio-based to trade type systems, and on order execution gets transferred and captured into a downstream blockchain-ed system for accounting, record keeping and custody. Throughout the process, a trade appears as a sequence of many statuses.

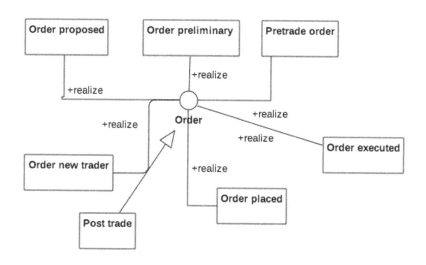

Figure 24 - Trade order management

Trade execution business scenario

The trade order management kicks off a trade wherein the contract goes through several such state changes. Some state changes occur fast, others take days to complete, from the time of the start of the client's decision to its initiation, execution and post-trade processing. A crude workflow as in figure 26 describes the intake of trade orders and their subsequent life cycle, starting from portfolio evaluation and analysis, order creation, trading to post-trade management.

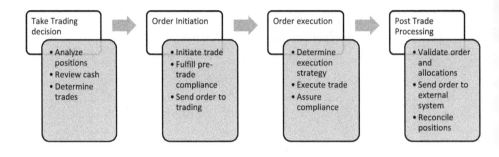

Figure 25 - Tasks and Sub-Tasks

To implement such services, here is a concise trade-order micro-service in JavaScript that can run with Node-JS. As with the other micro-services, this implementation is far from complete. The reader can complete the details and the implementation.

```
/*eslint-disable*/
/*jshint esversion: 6*/

let express = require('express');
let app = express();
let router = express.Router();

let tradeOrderEnum = {"PRELIMINARY":1,
    "PROPOSED":2, "PRETRADE":3,
    "NEWORDER":4, "PLACED":5,
    "EXECUTED":6, "POSTTRADE":7
};

Object.freeze(tradeOrderEnum)
```

```
var myLogger = function (req, res, next) {
  console.log('LOGGED')
  next()
}

router.use(function (req, res, next) {
  console.log('Time:', Date.now())
  next()
})

router.get('/initiate/:ordertype/:client', function (req, res, next) {
  let orderType = req.params.ordertype;
  switch (orderType) {
    case (tradeOrderEnum.EXECUTED):
        // do something
    case (tradeOrderEnum.NEWORDER):
        // do something
    case (tradeOrderEnum.PLACED):
        // do something
    case (tradeOrderEnum.POSTTRADE):
        // do something
    case (tradeOrderEnum.PRELIMINARY):
        // do something
    case (tradeOrderEnum.PRETRADE) :
        // do something
    case (tradeOrderEnum.PROPOSED) :
        // do something
    default: break;
  }
  console.log('Request URL:', req.originalUrl)
  console.log(req.params.client,
        req.params.ordertype)
  res.send({ 'Got it':
        'Trade order on its way' })
})
```

```
app.use('/tradeorder/', router)
app.use(myLogger)

console.log('Tradeorder Listening at port 9993')
app.listen(9993)
```

To run this service, execute the URL:

http://localhost:9993/tradeorder/initiate/2/001

Trading decisions

The thought of trading does not transpire unless the client agrees to a high-level investment strategy. That the client signs on the dotted line to begin investments is a clear signal to any trading activity. At this junction, benchmarking the customer's existing portfolio, the financial planning system primes the marching orders in conducting specific investments. Increasing or decreasing the exposures to any specific asset class may be part of the order. Based on the decision, some interesting questions arise - what specific adjustments in the current portfolio and what new trades can really meet the newfound goals. One can start by analyzing the positions and then move on to reviewing the cash required to fulfill the trade order. In analyzing positions, we can start by exploring the customer's current holdings and positions. Next, we can assess how much cash is available to execute the trades. Based on these findings, the order can undergo adjustments and tweaks. And at the third stage, the client needs the right facts on the trade order being compliant, secure and meeting the goals. This phase also offers a good opportunity to assess any tax situations.

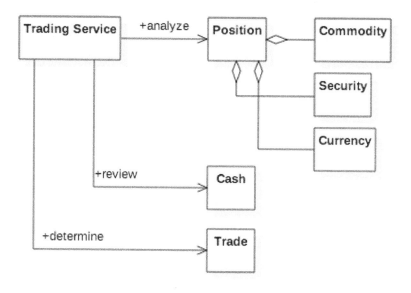

Figure 26 - Trade Decision

Commencing the trade order is by far not a simple task, the mix-and-match of stocks and asset-classes must be such as to reach the intended mark quickly. Bearing in mind the real time market and price data that offer a quick snapshot of the market conditions, the order gets created. Pre-trade compliance and verification is undeniably necessary and the trade order undergoes checks for vulnerabilities and loop-holes. If any signs of exception or warning come about, the client should be able to take suitable recourse to counteract them. The last step in this phase is in sending the orders to the trading desk for execution.

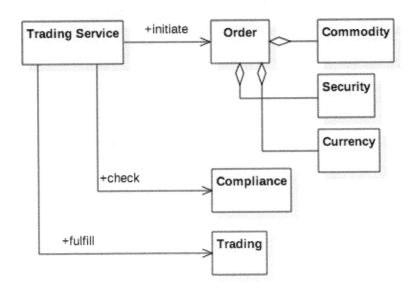

Figure 27 - Order Initiation

Order execution

A trading sub-system plays a key role in this phase of the workflow. It must first assume the ownership of the trade order it receives from the parent financial planning system. Trading system analyzes the fundamentals like price and volume to arrive at the best execution strategy for the trades it must execute. As such, the system reviews the commission details and costs, determines the broker and trading venues for the most efficient trade execution. It merges and splits the trades when needed for efficient execution. The system evaluates any cross-trading opportunities. Any strategy that can reckon the best execution of the trade order is given top priority. Whether creating placements, transmitting placements, or executing the order, the best-execution check is indispensable. Individual brokers or an execution management system receive the trades. Once complete, reviews are carried out on the execution to check for price anomalies. Sell orders are designated for taxes.

The trade order undergoes checks also for regulatory and policy compliances. Necessary action for any violation are notified, then reported and lodged into the blockchain.

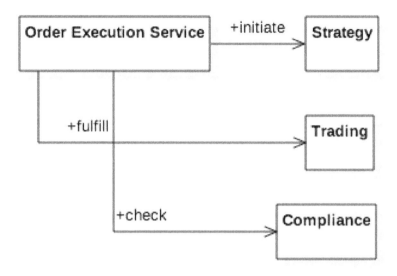

Figure 28 - Order Execution

Post-trade processing

Post trade processing and analysis is a primary requirement to ensure the order is compliant and its details maintained for any reconciliation later. Figure 29 illustrates the post trade activities.

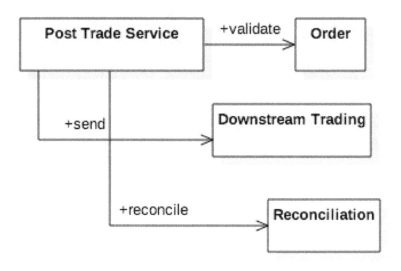

Figure 29 - Post Trade Processing

Post trade activities normally validate the orders and allocations. Matching the transactions to security, price, fees and currency is an elaborate exercise. It also includes reviewing the trade clearance, netting and settlement instructions. A blockchained system received the trade-order on completion. Results of reconciling the transactions, checking the positions and managing the cash balances is also a candidate for the blockchain database. Post trade activities such as reconciling often revisits the goals to gather metrics on whether the client or the advisory is on track to meet the goals. The service often uses constant expected returns or simulated returns from Monte Carlo Simulation.

Review, re-plan, re-balance, re-coup

To meet the needs of wealth management consulting and long-term customer relationships, the services outlined for customer review and re-planning sessions include services that can instantly analyze portfolio performance and risk, conduct simulations on-the-fly to re-plan and re-balance the portfolio when the goals change or fall short.

No matter how perfect the portfolio, there's little doubt that in a short time, the asset allocation is out of whack[30]. The stock market will have either shot upward, causing the stock allocation to run higher than planned, or it will have experienced a downturn, causing the allocation to be lower in value.

The reader may try some valuable third-party portfolio systems built around Node-JS and Python to test such scenarios.

Finance	https://www.npmjs.com /package/finance
Node-Portfolio	https://www.npmjs.com /package/portfolio
Python rebalance asset allocation	https://pypi.python.org /pypi/RebalanceAssetAllocation/0.1.2
Python asset allocation	https://github.com/skipperkongen/asset-allocation

Some years back, Monte Carlo simulation had become a popular method for simulating the range of possible outcomes in retail investment. It provided the investor with an understanding of the perceived risk taken over a certain period.

---

[30] https://obliviousinvestor.com/asset-allocation-and-risk-tolerance/ - Author Mike Piper

In options analysis, Monte Carlo methods construct "stochastic" or probabilistic financial models as opposed to the traditional static and deterministic models. In order to analyze the characteristics of a project's net present value - NPV, the cash flow components impacted by uncertainty get modeled, incorporating any correlations between the numbers, while mathematically reflecting their "random characteristics". Then, these results are combined in a histogram of NPV - the project's probability distribution, and the average NPV of the potential investment - as well as its volatility and other sensitivities - is observed. This distribution allows, for example, for an estimate of the probability that the project has a net present value greater than zero or any other value[31].

As the reader, you experienced Hyperledger with its several blockchain implementations offering a strong choice of architecture, let me summarize the features we covered. Hyperledger composer lets the parties define their "business network", a judiciously chosen gathering of people and machines whose goal serves the contract or agreement. The business network owes its definition to the artifacts and rules which are collected and digitized for different deployments. Several participants access the "business network", some even undertake to maintain it.

The maintainer of the network runs a good deal of hardware "peer nodes", sustaining the system. To prevent a crash, Hyperledger Fabric replicates the distributed ledger across such peer nodes. Composer modeling language expresses the domain model of the business network.

---

[31] https://en.wikipedia.org/wiki/Monte_Carlo_methods_in_finance

The model, once constructed, allows developers to capture "smart contracts" as 'executable transaction processor functions', written in JavaScript.

Hyperledger Sawtooth is the strong choice among nimble implementations with a powerful Burrow combination to enable the use of many Smart Contracts written for Ethereum. This chapter treated both architectures covering their strong points, besides extending into micro-services and other useful code. As this chapters comes to a close and we move into the new chasms of lending and mortgage, the next chapter though shorter in description, is not short on content. Much of Hyperledger Fabric and Sawtooth-Seth engineering and architecture were portrayed in this chapter.

MORTGAGE LOAN ORIGINATION AND BLOCKCHAIN

While it looked daunting in the beginning, I suffered a severe writer's block when I spun this manuscript at first in my head. But, no sooner had I come around to logically clubbing together the many disparate portions, I immediately sat down to write this manuscript. One thing I realized early, it was way too big to fit into one book, furthermore, the proof of technology presented significant challenges, so I trimmed the scope to just address the design and implementation of a mortgage loan processing and underwriting through a Fannie Mae overlay, all constrained within the distributed ledger world. In essence, this chapter lends to a real design and implementation and the code is available for download at GitHub.

The lending industry is grappling with low general demand, price inflation, credit tightening, rates trending upwards, high regulatory changes, customer demand for better experiences, the financial technology (FinTech) disruptors and incessant online security threats. Without doubt, automated underwriting technology continues to contribute to lower costs of origination. It is also true that only recently some lenders have begun to appreciate the results functional process automation can bring. From there, adopt end-to-end automated systems.

 **Demand and Supply**
The need for mortgages remains high, but lenders have to work harder to increase their relationships with customers, a clear sign that lending systems need to tap into data sources of different origins to establish good customer experiences.

Regardless of rising housing prices and unrest, many Americans still see the promise of investing in homes. Slowdowns do not necessarily stop home ownership. Then, efforts to increase the borrower base has led to home-buying opportunities for new consumer groups and the newer generation of buyers. Among the loan products, however, refinancing still remains the strongest. While lenders try to overcome the limitations of selling mortgage products through financial solutions, the value chain keeps expanding beyond just mortgages. Top originators know for certain that they have to rely on different channels to deliver their services in order to meet the demand for new loans. Major lenders have been trying to automate and secure their existing processes and improve overall business agility and flexibility in accommodating regulatory compliance.

We all understand one thing – Speed is the key.

Strangely, the loan origination process which only does loan processing and underwriting is one major area of the entire loan system that is devoid of speed. Old practices remain dominant leading to poor closing time and exorbitant closing costs. This is where blockchain comes to the rescue. While major lenders have shown signs of adopting workflow technologies to integrate servicing processes with origination and delivery, blockchain easily expands its territory to all this and beyond, even into real estate sales and post mortgage activities. Though several lenders have put an effort to automate workflows but still continue to use paper-based processes with zero orchestration, tracking and monitoring, the blockchain promise eliminates the reliance on paper trail.

 The time and money spent on mortgage origination is roughly 80% of what goes into the complete loan process. LOS is a complex process, centered on the loan application, its processing and underwriting. Freddie Mac form 65 or the Fannie Mae form 1003, now nicknamed URLA is a lengthy application, and exhaustive in the way it captures the borrowers' information, the agency involved, likely lender, application-type and information on the real estate. If loan-data were the center of the universe as shown in figure 30, what principally appears as icing on a cake are the credit services, escrow, insurance, property title and vendor order management. In essence, the FNM ULDD[32] or Uniform Loan Delivery Dataset supports the pattern - 'decorator'.

---

[32] https://www.fanniemae.com/singlefamily/uniform-loan-delivery-dataset-uldd

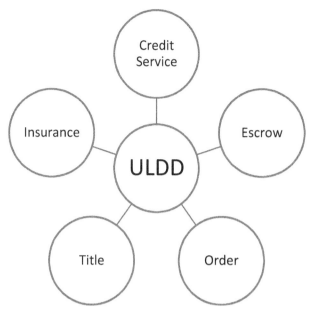

Figure 30 - ULDD/URLA

Those who have gone through the ordeals of home buying or refinancing know how lengthy and expensive the process of a mortgage loan is. What is puzzling - why is it so? Today, FNM provides the means to automated underwriting. Any software application can grab data from multiple resources and complete the FNM application at high speed. Then why isn't it happening? Imagine the costs borne by the borrowers and lenders can become nothing by using software services, distributed ledgers and nimble web services. It tells you nothing more than how disoriented and inefficient is the lending industry.

What is needed to architect such a loan origination system are functions and software services that collect score checks, credit verification, authorization, rate locks, underwriting, escrowing, property-appraisals, property-title-services, property-checks, funding and insurance.

Tenets of design

I have captured the mortgage-application process at a high-level using a UML class model in Figure 31. In the mortgage origination life cycle, there are several players and many tasks. The contract goes through several iterations, each time satisfying the lender, till a climactic point when the lender decides to fund the loan. Our stops at this junction, at the point when the underwriting is complete. The reader can appreciate that only speed, accuracy and completeness can achieve the best results. Only the lender and borrower are the ones who have a long way to go with the contract. Other participants are secondary, such as the realtor who manages listings and the sale of properties, the title agent who insures the title for the borrower, or the appraiser who provides an estimate on the real estate. Their roles are short-lived and never go beyond the property sale.

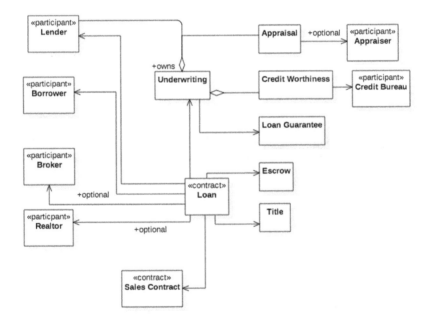

Figure 31 - Loan Originations Scope

The credit report is one tool used by brokers and lenders throughout the mortgage process, which helps to determine what loan programs the borrower may qualify for and how much loan is manageable by the person. The credit report lists the past payment history of the borrower and helps in determining the borrower's likelihood of making timely mortgage payments. Electronic versions of credit reports have become more commonly used in the mortgage industry in the last ten years. Earlier, people used to request credit reports by fax, mail or phone. Today, credit requests are transmitted as electronic transactions that use either proprietary or public data formats. In the last few years, the MISMO XML format has become the accepted standard among lenders and credit bureaus as a standard in lending application.

Pre-approved mortgage is still another subject to review once the buyer selects a specific property, so guaranteeing the dollar amount may occur later. There is even the possibility of a pre-approved loan getting reduced or revoked. Especially, if the lender gets the slightest hint that the property in question is unsellable because of preconditions, location constraints or other factors. With preapproval, a borrower receives a conditional commitment for an exact loan amount, allowing the borrower to look for a home at or below that price level. This puts the borrower at an advantage when dealing with a potential seller, as the seller knows the borrower is one step closer to obtaining an actual mortgage.

As a Listing Agent,	
I would like to list a real estate property on behalf of a seller. I would like to accurately classify the property, maintain interested party records, identify a buyer and pass the information to the lender to take it from there.	
Expected outcome:	A listing, I can monitor.
Failed outcome:	A listing that will not fetch a buyer or mortgage.

As a Lender,	
I would like to rapidly on-board a client, understand his quest for a property purchase and get the loan underwritten by Fannie Mae or Freddie Mac within minutes. I need to preserve the transactions from the point the client visits the real estate and agrees to its purchase, to the loan for the sale being processed and ready to be underwritten.	
Expected outcome:	All such transactions, I and the client can monitor - up to automated underwriting.
Failed outcome:	Failed underwriting.
Pre-conditions:	Signed agreement by seller and buyer
Post-conditions	Close the loan and either maintain the portfolio or sell the loan to third party.

We can design the Mortgage Application URLA[33] (*Uniform Residential Loan Application*) to run as a web service on top of a blockchain database. Combining the power of Node.JS and Hyperledger Fabric, we can safely erect the architecture of a loan origination micro-service. A broad definition of a micro-service is they have a single responsibility. Such services assume the accountability of one part of the domain and diligently share that information as a source of truth. They offer an API of interfaces some of which are in human readable format, the remaining meant for other machines.

Repeating as we had done with the financial planning use-case, our journey into the making of a lending micro-service starts by demarcating a business network. Though the name I have suggested is generic, you may consider a more specific description. The name-space comes next. A proper name-space maintains the focus when many networks exist. The name-space allows similar functionality to exist in different name-spaces.

On a different terminal window either through Visual Studio Code or by using standard MacOS or Ubuntu terminal, make a new directory, change to that directory and run the Yeoman CLI.

```
$ mkdir mortgage-los
$ cd mortgage-los

$ yo hyperledger-composer:businessnetwork
```

---

[33] https://www.fanniemae.com/singlefamily/uniform-residential-loan-application

```
Welcome to the business network generator
? Business network name: mortgage-los
? Description: Mortgage LOS
? Author name:  Dev B
? Author email: devb@linux.com
? License: Apache-2.0
? Namespace: com.devb.mortgage
  create index.js
  ...
```

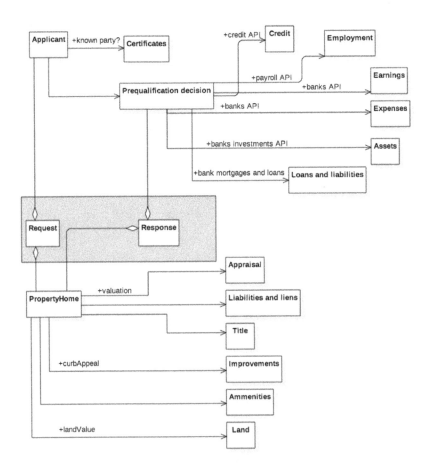

Figure 32 - Prequalification RESTful interface for request/response

Think of our service having two outfits – one collects data, the other stores relevant information. Collecting documents in electronic, blockchain-ed or PDF format is not a trivial task. Since a smart contract for document management is our aim for the book, the hashed-data of such documents can be stored in protected blocks without worrying about version-ing and history.

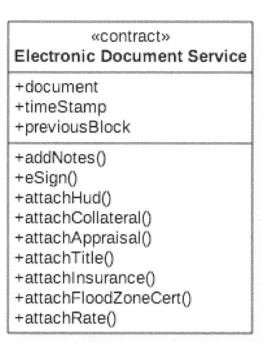

Figure 33 – Electronic document - Smart Contract

The service in Figure 33 is a generalized one that gathers documents, collaterals, appraisals and stores their hash code in the Blockchain. Should a dispute rise years later, the hash-code and the time stamp would be the proof that such documents were part of the service earlier.

It is hard to foretell what the law will be, there are several lawmakers looking into the possibility of blockchain becoming the next transaction system and therefore investigating how the new laws would emerge for such systems.

Designing the Ledger Model

All artifacts that drive the mortgage business stem from a model-driven design appropriate to one suggested for Hyperledger. Though we have quickly moved to a concrete design as shown in Figure 34, much of the design comes from the MISMO standards that are prevalent today. Like the financial planning system, lending is a well-known activity, and some proven methods exist today. Imagine if you were to build a lending system from scratch – in our case, the initial design that began as user stories, which graduated to a white-board, found its way into the blockchain ecosystem.

URLA design adheres to the standards set by MISMO for the Fannie Mae ULDD/URLA messages. You may notice the class model in Figure 34 runs a deep nested object tree. The design is the three-object design between Person, Asset and Product. Transferred are assets between persons through a product or contract – in this case the Mortgage Loan. The life-cycle of a real estate sale or transfer is a rather convoluted process involving many players. Initial transactions begin with the seller, realtor, the buyer and a few agents. A parallel phase begins when the buyer needs funds and the lender gets involved. After the mortgage closing, much of the involved parties disappears from the network, leaving the original lender and the buyer and the potential to sell the loan to another lender.

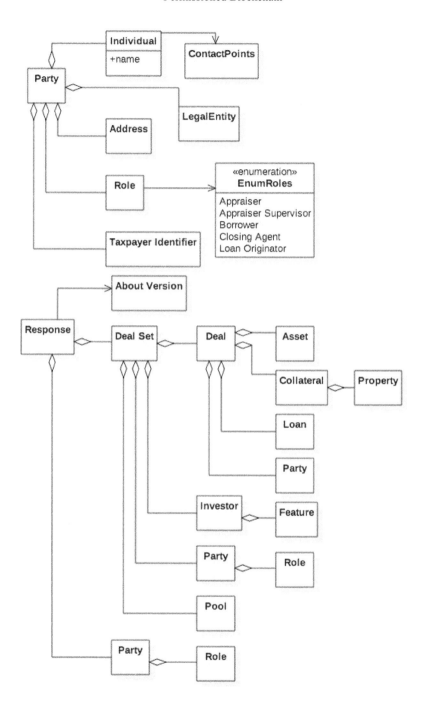

Figure 34 - RESTful model for application

 To manage such a large set of transactions, I have created a Hyperledger Composer model that captures many of the nuances.

```
namespace com.devb.mortgage
```

The *PersonRoleType* is an enumeration of the different roles that take part in a typical mortgage contract. Some roles, you can well imagine, may not even apply in a permissioned network.

```
enum PersonRoleType {
  o ASSET_OWNER
  o APPRAISER
  o APPRAISER_SUPERVISOR
  o BORROWER
  o BUYER
  o DOCUMENT_CUSTODIAN
  o HOMEOWNERS_ASSOCIATION
  o LISTING_AGENT
  o LOAN_DELIVERY_FILE_PREPARER
  o LOAN_ORIGINATION_COMPANY
  o LOAN_ORIGINATOR
  o LOAN_SELLER
  o LENDER
  o NOTE_PAY_TO
  o OTHER
  o PAYEE
  o PROPERTY_SELLER
  o REALTOR
  o SELLER
  o SERVICER
  o WAREHOUSE_LENDER
}
```

PropertyType is another enumeration like people type, it classifies different real estate types. The list describes what exists today and opens the room for further expansion. While the contract's intent keeps it confined to residential loans, extending to incorporate other types like schools and offices is easy.

```
enum PropertyType {
  o SINGLE_FAMILY
  o CONDOMINIUM
  o APARTMENT
  o MULTIPLE_FAMILY
  o PREFABRICATED
  o MOBILE_HOME
}
```

Real estate selling is a state engine where the life-cycle varies from listed to active, to closed or expired.

```
enum PropertyStandardStatus {
  o LISTED
  o ACTIVE
  o ACTIVE_UNDER_CONTRACT
  o PENDING
  o HOLD
  o WITHDRAWN
  o CLOSED
  o EXPIRED
  o CANCELED
  o DELETE
  o INCOMPLETE
  o COMING_SOON
}
```

Listed are different loan types in the 'LoanTypes' enumeration. Loan products based on the loan types offer more versatility. Depending on the lender and products they offer, this enumeration can undergo adjustments.

```
enum LoanTypes {
  o ADJUSTMENT
  o ARM
  o AFFORDABLE_LENDING
  o AMORTIZATION
  o BUYDOWN
  o CONSTRUCTION
  o CREDIT_ENHANCEMENTS
  o DRAW
  o FHA
  o FIXED_15
  o FIXED_30
  o GOVERNMENT_LOAN
  o HELOC
  o HMDA_LOAN
  o INTEREST_ONLY
  o REFINANCE
  o RESPA
  o USDA
  o VA
}
```

Like the real estate, the loan goes through several processes and states.

```
enum LoanStatusType {
  o NONE
  o AT_CLOSING
  o AT_MODIFICATION
  o AT_CLOSING_NON_MOD
  o AT_CLOSING_MOD
  o AT_CONVERSION
  o AT_RESET
  o CURRENT
}
enum LoanRoleType {
  o SUBJECT_LOAN
  o RELATED_LOAN
}
concept OtherAsset {
  o String assetId
  o String assetName
}
```

The Property-Home describes the real estate that is being listed. I have deliberately kept the property-title and appraisal away from this asset code to reduce complexity of the contract. Real estate, an asset will possess a registry in Fabric.

```
asset PropertyHome identified by propertyId {
  o String propertyId
  o String propertyName
  o PropertyType propertyType
  o PropertyStandardStatus propertyState
  o Boolean isListed optional
  --> Person listingAgent
  o String address
  o String city
  o String state
  o String zip
  o Double value
  o DateTime listingStart
  o DateTime listingEnd
}
```

The Escrowbook is a short-term asset maintained by a trusted keeper during the property sale and perhaps after funding the loan.

```
asset EscrowBook identified by escrowId {
  o String escrowId
  --> PropertyHome home
  --> Person buyer
  --> Person keeper
  o Double sellValue
  o Double downPayment
  o Double heldInEscrow
  o Double promisedPayment
  o Double mortgagePayment
  o String document
}
```

These concepts and assets are applied in the Fannie Mae Freddie Mac ULDD or URLA construct.

```
                                          ● ● Composer

concept Loan {
  o String loanId
  o LoanTypes loanType
  o String investorFeature optional
  o String loanComments
  o String loanDetail
  o String loanLevelCredit
  o String loanPrograms
  o LoanStatusType loanState
  o Double ltv
  o String maturity
  o String mers_registrations
  o String mi_data
  o String modifications
  o String optional_products
  o Double payment
  o String prepayment_Penalty
  o String qualification
  o String servicing
  o String termsOfMortgage
  o String underwriting
}

concept Deal {
  o String dealId
  o OtherAsset otherAsset optional
  --> PropertyHome collateral optional
  o Loan loan
  o Double combinedLTV
  --> Party partyRoles
}
concept DealSet {
  o String dealSetId
  o Deal deal
  --> Person investorFeature
  --> Party partyRoles optional
  o String pool
}
```

```
concept DealSets {
  o String dealSetsId
  o DealSet dealSet
  --> Party partyRoles optional
  o ULDDGovernmentMonitoring ulddGovtMonitoring
}

concept ULDDGovernmentMonitoring {
  o String ulddGovtId
  o String hmdaEthnicity
  o String hmdaEthnicityOrigin
  o String hmdaRaceDesignation
  o String hmdaRaceDetail
}

asset ULDD30 identified by loanId {
  o String loanId
  o LoanTypes loadIdType
  o String aboutVersion
  o DealSets dealSets
}

participant Party identified by partyId {
  o String partyId
  --> Person[] persons
  o ContactPoint[] contactPoint
  o String name
  o Address[] address
  o PersonRoleType role
  o String taxIdentifier
}

concept ContactPoint {
  o String contactId
  o String contactPoint
}

concept Address {
  o String addressId
  o String addressLine1
  o String addressLine2
  o String city
  o String state
  o String postalCode
}
```

```
participant Person identified by personId {
  o String personId
  o PersonRoleType personRoleType
  o String governmentId
  o String firstName
  o String lastName
}

transaction ListProperty {
  --> PropertyHome home
  o Boolean listed
}

transaction Revalue {
  --> PropertyHome home
  o String newValue
}

transaction GenerateULDD {
  --> ULDD30 fnmOverlay
}
transaction Escrow {
  --> EscrowBook escrowBook
  --> Person buyer
  o Double money
  o String document
}

event OtherEvent {
  --> PropertyHome home
  o Double oldValue
  o Double newValue
}
```

One of the primary aims of the model is to ensure the data that goes into the blockchain adheres to the requirements of standards bodies like RESO (Real Estate Standards Organization) and MISMO (Mortgage Standards). With Fannie Mae increasing its footage in automated underwriting, it is often easier for lenders and banks to send the data directly to Fannie Mae or Freddie Mac and get a quick underwriting of the loan.

One can start with Hyperledger Composer and set the grounds for deploying the contract. If you recall, the first thing after creating the contract is program archiving all artifacts into a BNA (*business network archive*).

```
$ composer archive create -t dir -n .
```
```
Creating Business Network Archive
Looking for package.json of Business Network
Definition
        Input directory: /Users/[user]/Blockchain/h-
composer/mortgage-los/mortgage-los
Found:
        Description: Mortgage LOS
        Name: mortgage-los
        Identifier: mortgage-los@0.0.1

Written Business Network Definition Archive file to
        Output file: mortgage-los@0.0.1.bna
Command succeeded
```

```
$ composer runtime install --card PeerAdmin@hlfv1 --
businessNetworkName mortgage-los
```
```
✔   Installing runtime for business network mortgage-
los. This may take a minute...
Command succeeded

// This command changes in Fabric v 1.11
```
```
$ composer network install --archiveFile mortgage-los@0.0.1.bna
--card PeerAdmin@hlfv1
```

```
$ composer network start --card PeerAdmin@hlfv1 --
networkAdmin admin --networkAdminEnrollSecret adminpw --
archiveFile mortgage-los@0.0.1.bna --file networkadmin.card
```
```
Starting business network from archive: mortgage-
los@0.0.1.bna
Business network definition:
        Identifier: mortgage-los@0.0.1
        Description: Mortgage LOS
Processing these Network Admins:
        userName: admin
```

```
✔  Starting business network definition. This may
take a minute...
Successfully created business network card:
        Filename: networkadmin.card

Command succeeded

// This command changes in Fabric v 1.11
// The network version must match the BND
```

$ composer network start --networkName mortgage-los --
networkVersion 0.0.1 --card PeerAdmin@hlfv1 --networkAdmin
admin --networkAdminEnrollSecret adminpw

```
// In Fabric 1.11, it will generate
// admin@mortgage-los.card
// Change the name of the card accordingly
```

$ composer card import --file networkadmin.card

```
Successfully imported business network card
        Card file: networkadmin.card
        Card name: admin@mortgage-los

Command succeeded
```

$ composer network ping --card admin@mortgage-los

```
The connection to the network was successfully
tested: mortgage-los
        version: 0.16.6
        participant:
org.hyperledger.composer.system.NetworkAdmin#admin

Command succeeded
```

The composer REST server provides all the API to interact with the business network and the underlying blockchain.

$ composer-rest-server

```
? Enter the name of the business network card to use:
networkadmin.card
```

```
? Specify if you want namespaces in the generated
REST API: never use namespaces
? Specify if you want to enable authentication for
the REST API using Passport: No
? Specify if you want to enable event publication
over WebSockets: No
? Specify if you want to enable TLS security for the
REST API: No
To restart the REST server using the same options,
issue the following command:
composer-rest-server -c networkadmin.card -n never
```

In the home selling use case, fetched is data from different sources on the borrower and the property (home), bringing the two together through a loan product to arrive at a Fannie Mae/Freddie Mac ULDD construct. The regulatory body of MISMO (Mortgage Industry Standards Maintenance Organization), a subsidiary of MBA (Mortgage Bankers Association) defines the specifications required for a standardized residential loan. Those familiar with loan originations, will comprehend that loan processing + underwriting comprises the bulk of work, often exceeding 80 percent of the load. Regarding funding and closing processes - though it takes a while in bringing a mortgage loan process to a finish; these functions are proprietary and discretionary.

The proposed mortgage engine provides a uniform system of engagement that can:
- Generate gains in user and design productivity and innovation by eliminating the impacts of process, information and system fragmentation.
- Reduce the time to build and lower total cost of ownership of systems by providing frameworks, tools and services that promote and speed up convergence toward implementation standards.

To accomplish the above goal in architecting the mortgage engine, I considered different architectural goals and decisions during the design process.

- Setting a unified framework for all mortgage-related services, application program interfaces (API) and work management.
  - Single-entry point for multiple access channels into the blockchain
  - Standard building tools for application development

The solution is largely model driven to ensure a common way to communicate requirements, architecture and design. It is a series of progressive elaborations that:

- Maintain alignment between expectations and implementation
- Promote consistency and effective implementation of the described methods
- Serve as a guide to other projects

In the book, I have deferred any interconnection between the financial planning and the lending for later. What I have included is the URLA software in Python as it provides a definite conclusion to both Financial Planning and Lending.

As a Lender,	
I would like to quickly create a RESO/MISMO compliant application I can render into a blockchain to have the data replicated on different agency nodes such as federal loan agencies, Fannie Mae or Freddie Mac or just fund it myself.	
Expected outcome:	A URLA I can revisit and monitor.
Failed outcome:	A bad URLA that will not be eligible for a loan.

The folder structure gives you an idea on how to assemble the software-application.

```
+ mortgage_urla
__init__.py
index.py
readme.md
install.md
app.yaml
    + com
        __init__.py
        + devb
            __init__.py
            + mortgage
                __init__.py
                + urla
                    UrlaResource.py
```

The python file contains the REST resources required by the loan-application client. It caters to the URLA requirements yet optimized for storage. The output produced may not be exactly as in the URLA XML format. The application in Python 3.4 generates the Mortgage URLA from various inputs and stores the loan-application in a blockchain. It requires data from the financial planning to complete the mortgage-application.

```
#!/usr/bin/env python
#  * @author Devb
#  * @License Apache 2.0
#  * consolidated_client.py
```

Unlike JavaScript, JSON is an external entity to Python code. To encode in JSON, the json library comes handy.

```
import json
from datetime import date
from json import JSONEncoder
```

Flask libraries offer a strong REST / API and Resource libraries for generating middleware code.

```
from flask.helpers import make_response
from flask_restful import Api, Resource
import base64

def enum(**enums):
    return type('Enum', (), enums)
```

Within the code, the encode and decode functions provide a strong encryption on any sensitive data such as SSN and Phone numbers. The JSON itself can undergo hashing before they are sent to the blockchain.

```
def encode(key, clear):
    enc = []
    for i in range(len(clear)):
        key_c = key[i % len(key)]
        enc_c = chr((ord(clear[i]) + ord(key_c)) % 256)
        enc.append(enc_c)
    return base64.urlsafe_b64encode("".join(enc).encode())
                                          .decode()

def decode(key, enc):
    dec = []
    enc = base64.urlsafe_b64decode(enc).decode()
    for i in range(len(enc)):
        key_c = key[i % len(key)]
        dec_c = chr((256 + ord(enc[i]) -
                ord(key_c)) % 256)
        dec.append(dec_c)
    return "".join(dec)


# Enums
EstateHeld = enum(FEESIMPLE='FEESIMPLE',
            LEASEHOLD='LEASEHOLD')
BorrowerEnum = enum(BORROWER='BORROWER',
            CO_BORROWER='CO_BORROWER')
AddressEnum = enum(
    CURRENT_ADDRESS='CURRENT_ADDRESS',
    PREV_ADDRESS='PREV_ADDRESS',
    WORK_ADDRESS='WORK_ADDRESS',
    COMMERCIAL_ADDRESS='COMMERCIAL_ADDRESS')
```

```
Ethnicity = enum(WHITE='WHITE',
        AFRICAN_AMERICAN='AFRICAN_AMERICAN',
        ASIAN='ASIAN',
        HISPANIC='HISPANIC',
        LATINO='LATINO',
        MIDDLE_EAST='MIDDLE_EAST')
Gender = enum(
        MALE='MALE', FEMALE='FEMALE',
        UNKNOWN='UNKNOWN')
MaritalStatus = enum(
        MARRIED='MARRIED',
        SINGLE='SINGLE', DIVORCED='DIVORCED',
        WIDOWED='WIDOWED')
Improvement_Type = enum(
        CHANGES_MADE='CHANGES_MADE',
        CHANGES_TOBEMADE='CHANGES_TOBEMADE',
        NONE='NONE')
PropertyTypeEnum = enum(
   INVESTMENT_PROPERTY='INVESTMENT_PROPERTY',
   PRINCIPAL_RESIDENCE='PRINCIPAL_RESIDENCE',
   SECOND_HOME='SECOND_HOME',
   NOT_SPECIFIED='NOT_SPECIFIED')
PurposeTypeEnum = enum(
   CONSTRUCTION='CONSTRUCTION',
   CONSTRUCTION_PERMANENT='CONSTRUCTION_PERMANENT',
   PURCHASE='PURCHASE',
   REFINANCE='REFINANCE',
   OTHER='OTHER')
# End Enums
```

The example secret key is used for encoding and decoding the sensitive data.

```
secret_key = '1234567890123456'
```

The 'Urla' class needs sets of information from different sources to complete the FNM compliant URLA. The classes mostly appear alphabetically with a few exceptions.

```python
# DEF CLASS
class AlimonyChildSupport(object):
    monthlyPayment = float()
    monthsLeft = float()
    owedTo = None

    def __init__(self):

        """ method __init__ """
# UNDEF CLASS

# DEF CLASS
class AddressType(object):
    address_1 = None
    address_2 = None
    city = None
    numberYears = int()
    state = None
    zipCode = int()
    propertyType = None
    numberYears = int()

    def __init__(self):
        """ method __init__ """

# UNDEF CLASS
```

```
# DEF CLASS
class AssetType(object):
    amount = float()
    description = None

    def __init__(self):
        """ method __init__ """
# UNDEF CLASS
```

The 'assets and liabilities' class is an important object tree containing other objects like alimony child support, checking and savings details, real estate, life insurance, stocks and bonds and others.

```
# DEF CLASS
class AssetsLiabilities(object):
    alimonyChildSupport = AlimonyChildSupport()
    asset = AssetType()
    automobile = None
    businessOwned = float()
    cashDeposit = None
    checkingSavings = None
    creditPrevious = None
    jobRelatedExpense = None
    liability = None
    lifeInsurance = None
    realEstate = None
    realEstateOwned = float()
    retirementFund = float()
    stocksBonds = None
    def __init__(self):
        """ method __init__ """
# UNDEF CLASS
```

```
# DEF CLASS
class AutomobileType(object):
    amount = float()
    autoSequence = int()
    description = None

    def __init__(self):
        """ method __init__ """
# UNDEF CLASS
```

The Borrower type defines the main borrower and the co-borrower. The application can encrypt all sensitive data belonging to the borrower before storing them.

```
# DEF CLASS
class BorrowerType(object):
    address = []  # list of addresstype
    borrower = None
    dateOfBirth = date
    declarations = None
    dependents = []
    employment = None
    firstName = None
    governmentMonitoring = None
    income = None
    lastName = None
    maritalStatus = None
    middleName = None
    title = None
    yearsSchool = int()
    phone = None
    ssn = None
```

```python
    def __init__(self):
        """ method __init__ """

    def setssn(self, value):
        self.ssn = encode(secret_key,
                    str(value))

    def getssn(self, value):
        return decode(secret_key, self.ssn)

    def setphone(self, newphone):
        self.phone = encode(secret_key, str(newphone))

    def getphone(self, value):
        return decode(secret_key, self.phone)
# UNDEF CLASS

# DEF CLASS
class CashDepositType(object):
    amount = float()
    description = None

    def __init__(self):
        """ method __init__ """
# UNDEF CLASS

# DEF CLASS
class CheckingSavingsAccount(object):
    accountNumber = None
    accountSequence = int()
    bankAddress = AddressType()

    def __init__(self):
        """ method __init__ """
# UNDEF CLASS
```

```python
# DEF CLASS
class ConstructionType(object):
    amountExistingLiens = float()
    costOfImprovements = float()
    originalCost = float()
    presentValueOfLot = float()
    yearLotAcquired = int()

    def __init__(self):
        """ method __init__ """
# UNDEF CLASS

# DEF CLASS
class CreditReceivedType(object):
    accountNumber = None
    alternateName = None
    creditorName = None

    def __init__(self):
        """ method __init__ """
# UNDEF CLASS

# DEF CLASS
class DeclarationsType(object):
    anyJudgments = bool()
    borrowedDownPayment = bool()
    coMakerNote = bool()
    declaredBankrupt = bool()
    delinquent = bool()
    lawsuit = bool()
    obligatedOnAnyLoan = bool()
    obligatedToPayAlimony = bool()
    ownershipInterest = bool()
    permanentResident = bool()
    primaryResidence = bool()
    propertyForeclosed = bool()
```

```
    propertyType = None
    titleHeld = None
    uS_Citizen = bool()

    def __init__(self):
        """ method __init__ """
# UNDEF CLASS

# DEF CLASS
class Dependents(object):
    age = float()
    name = None

    def __init__(self):
        """ method __init__ """
# UNDEF CLASS

# DEF CLASS
class EmploymentType(object):
    businessPhone = None
    dateFrom = None
    dateTo = None
    employer = None
    isSelfEmployed = bool()
    monthlyIncome = float()
    position = None
    title = None
    typeOfBusiness = None
    yearsInProfession = float()

    def __init__(self):
        """ method __init__ """
# UNDEF CLASS
```

```python
# DEF CLASS
class Employer(object):
    address = []
    name = None

    def __init__(self):
        """ method __init__ """
# UNDEF CLASS

# DEF CLASS
class ExpenseType(object):
    firstMortgage = float()
    hazardInsurance = float()
    homeownersAssnDues = float()
    mortgageInsurance = float()
    other = float()
    otherFinancing = float()
    realEstateTaxes = float()
    rent = float()

    def __init__(self):
        """ method __init__ """
# UNDEF CLASS

# DEF CLASS
class GovernmentMonitoringType(object):
    race = Ethnicity
    sex = Gender

    def __init__(self):
        """ method __init__ """
# UNDEF CLASS
```

```python
# DEF CLASS
class IncomeType(object):
    baseEmployment = float()
    bonuses = float()
    commissions = float()
    dividendsInterest = float()
    netRentalIncome = float()
    other1 = float()
    other2 = float()
    otherIncome = None
    otherIncomeSources = float()
    overtime = float()

    def __init__(self):
        """ method __init__ """
# UNDEF CLASS
# DEF CLASS
class JobRelatedExpenseType(object):
    description = None
    monthlyPayment = float()
    monthsLeft = int()

    def __init__(self):
        """ method __init__ """
# UNDEF CLASS
# DEF CLASS
class LiabilityType(object):
    accountNumber = None
    address = None
    isToBePaidOff = bool()
    liabilitySequence = int()
    monthlyPayment = float()
    monthsLeft = int()
    name = None
    unpaidBalance = float()
```

```
    def __init__(self):
        """ method __init__ """
# UNDEF CLASS

# DEF CLASS
class LifeInsurance(object):
    faceAmount = float()
    netCashvalue = float()

    def __init__(self):
        """ method __init__ """
# UNDEF CLASS

# DEF CLASS
class OtherCreditType(object):
    amount = float()
    description = None

    def __init__(self):
        """ method __init__ """
# UNDEF CLASS

# DEF CLASS
class OtherIncomeType(object):
    amount = float()
    description = None

    def __init__(self):
        """ method __init__ """
# UNDEF CLASS
```

The PropertyType class along with the RealEstatePropertyType are used for real estate information.

```python
# DEF CLASS
class PropertyType(object):
    address1 = None
    address2 = None
    city = None
    county = None
    legalDescription = None
    numberOfUnits = int()
    state = None
    yearBuilt = int()
    zipCode = int()

    def __init__(self):
        """ method __init__ """
# UNDEF CLASS
```

The 'Purpose' class describes the purpose of the loan. There ae other classes like 'refinance type' which go into more specifics. This is required by the lender and FNM to determine the loan qualification.

```python
# DEF CLASS
class PurposeType(object):
    construction = None
    estateHeld = None
    estateHeldDescription = None
    mannerTitleHeld = None
    purposeType = None
    refinance = None
    sourceOfDownPayment = None
```

```
      titleHolderName = None
      typeDescription = None

      def __init__(self):
         """ method __init__ """
# UNDEF CLASS
# DEF CLASS
class RealEstatePropertyType(object):
      address = None
      grossRental = float()
      insuranceMisc = float()
      marketValue = float()
      mortgageLiens = float()
      mortgagePayments = float()
      netRental = float()
      propertySequence = int()
      status = None
      type_ = None

      def __init__(self):
         """ method __init__ """
# UNDEF CLASS
# DEF CLASS
class RefinanceType(object):
      amountExistingLiens = float()
      improvementCost = float()
      improvements = float()
      improvementType = None
      originalCost = float()
      purpose = None
      yearAcquired = int()

      def __init__(self):
         """ method __init__ """
# UNDEF CLASS
```

```python
# DEF CLASS
class StocksBondsAccountType(object):
    accountSequence = int()
    amount = float()
    description = None

    def __init__(self):
        """ method __init__ """
# UNDEF CLASS

# DEF CLASS
class TransactType(object):
    alterationsImprovements = float()
    closingCosts = float()
    closingCostsSeller = float()
    discount = float()
    land = float()
    loanAmount = float()
    otherCreditType = OtherCreditType()
    pmi_MIP = float()
    pmi_MIP_Financed = float()
    prepaidItems = float()
    purchasePrice = float()
    refinance = float()
    subordinateFinancing = float()

    def __init__(self):
        """ method __init__ """
# UNDEF CLASS
```

The Urla is the main mortgage-application class. It has several methods of converting to JSON formats. It uses a helper function Mortgage Json handler to serialize the JSON object.

```
# MAIN CLASS
# DEF CLASS
class Urla(object):
    agencyCaseNumber = None
    amortizationTypeDescription = None
    amount = float()
    applicationID = None
    dateCreated = None
    interestRate = float()
    lenderCaseNumber = None
    numberOfMonths = int()
    otherIncomeIncluded = bool()
    otherLiabilitiesIncluded = bool()
    residentialproperty = None
    purpose = PurposeType()
    representativeId = int()
    sourceIdentifier = None
    transactionType = None
    typeDescription = None
    borrower = BorrowerType()
    coborrower = BorrowerType()
    assetLiabilities = None
    employment = None

    def __init__(self):
        ''' method __init__ '''

    def toJSON(self):
        instDict = json.dumps(self.__dict__, sort_keys=False,
                    default=mortgage_json_handler)
        return instDict
```

```
    def tojjson(self):
      resp = make_response(json.dumps(self.__dict__,
           sort_keys=False, default=mortgage_json_handler))
      return resp

    def output_json(self, code, headers=None):
      resp = make_response(json.dumps(self), code)
      resp.headers.extend(headers or {})
      return resp
# UNDEF CLASS

def mortgage_json_handler(x):
    if isinstance(x, date):
      return x.isoformat()
    if isinstance(x, AddressType):
      return x.__dict__
    if isinstance(x, AlimonyChildSupport):
      return x.__dict__
    if isinstance(x, AssetsLiabilities):
      return x.__dict__
    if isinstance(x, AssetType):
      return x.__dict__
    if isinstance(x, BorrowerType):
      return x.__dict__
    if isinstance(x, CashDepositType):
      return x.__dict__
    if isinstance(x, CheckingSavingsAccount):
      return x.__dict__
    if isinstance(x, ConstructionType):
      return x.__dict__
    if isinstance(x, CreditReceivedType):
      return x.__dict__
    if isinstance(x, DeclarationsType):
      return x.__dict__
    if isinstance(x, Dependents):
      return x.__dict__
```

```
    if isinstance(x, EmploymentType):
        return x.__dict__
    if isinstance(x, Employer):
        return x.__dict__
    if isinstance(x, ExpenseType):
        return x.__dict__
    if isinstance(x, GovernmentMonitoringType):
        return x.__dict__
    if isinstance(x, IncomeType):
        return x.__dict__
    if isinstance(x, JobRelatedExpenseType):
        return x.__dict__
    if isinstance(x, LifeInsurance):
        return x.__dict__
    if isinstance(x, OtherCreditType):
        return x.__dict__
    if isinstance(x, OtherIncomeType):
        return x.__dict__
    if isinstance(x, PropertyType):
        return x.__dict__
    if isinstance(x, PurposeType):
        return x.__dict__
    if isinstance(x, RefinanceType):
        return x.__dict__
    if isinstance(x, StocksBondsAccountType):
        return x.__dict__
    if isinstance(x, TransactType):
        return x.__dict__
    raise TypeError(str(x) + " Unknown type")
# the end
```

There are numerous classes declared in one python service, which is turn runs the single responsibility of generating and maintaining the loan-application. The resource uses JSON, date-time, flask RESTful (API and Resource handlers) and the flask helper library.

Urla is the main class that assimilates the information. As in a decorator pattern, the Urla class is assisted by additional classes like Borrower, Assets and Liabilities, Property-type and many others. It also engages JSON handlers to represent itself as a proper request and response. The next python unit is the server that provides APIs to the external world.

```
#!/usr/bin/env python
#  * @author Devb
#  * @License Apache 2.0
import logging
import time
from datetime import date, datetime
from flask import Flask
from flask.helpers import make_response
from flask_restful import Api, Resource
import urllib.request
import random
```

The mortgage web service starts at this point. It uses the mortgage resource library. Routing, mediation and management of all invocations are carried out within. The GET method has a sample Urla class instantiation. It fills the instance with hard coded data. However, it could well use different APIs from external service providers to complete the class. You can check out the Node-RED flows[34] for solutions on using Node-JS to access payroll providers, Zillow and Bing (cognitive search on Azure)[35].

---

[34] https://flows.nodered.org/flow/0d46e43ee8a72cc15de43936648c1e9f
[35] https://flows.nodered.org/flow/7facb08800d13c4680c9d2a70edab98a

```python
from com.devb.mortgage.urla.UrlaResource import *

app = Flask(__name__)
api = Api(app)

@app.route('/')
@api.representation('application/json')
class UrlaService(Resource):

    def get(self, appid):
        mortgageApp = Urla()

        # property type
        propertyType = PropertyType()
        propertyType.address1 = "24 Blackhole Dr"
        propertyType.address2 = ""
        propertyType.city = "Newton"
        propertyType.state = "NJ"
        propertyType.yearBuilt = 1990
        propertyType.legalDescription = "Colonial, east facing
                property 16, lot 18"
        propertyType.numberOfUnits = 2
        propertyType.county = ""
        propertyType.zipCode = "07870"
        mortgageApp.property = propertyType
        purposeType = PurposeType()
        # construction
        constructionType = ConstructionType()
        constructionType.amountExistingLiens = 90000.00
        constructionType.costOfImprovements = 22335.68
        constructionType.originalCost = 160000.00
        constructionType.presentValueOfLot = 190000.00
        constructionType.yearLotAcquired = 1976
```

```
# purpose
purposeType.construction = constructionType
purposeType.estateHeld = EstateHeld.FEESIMPLE
purposeType.estateHeldDescription = "Held in simple way"
purposeType.mannerTitleHeld = None
purposeType.purposeType = PurposeTypeEnum.PURCHASE
# refinance
refinanceType = RefinanceType()
refinanceType.amountExistingLiens = 32000.0
refinanceType.improvementCost = 21000.00
refinanceType.improvements = 12000.00
refinanceType.improvementType =
      Improvement_Type.CHANGES_MADE
refinanceType.originalCost = 21000.00
refinanceType.purpose = "Curb side improvement"
refinanceType.yearAcquired = 1998
purposeType.refinance = refinanceType
purposeType.sourceOfDownPayment = "Bank financing"
purposeType.titleHolderName = "Joe Smith"
purposeType.typeDescription = "Refinance for Improvement"

# transaction type
tranType = TransactType()
tranType.alterationsImprovements = 2500.32
tranType.closingCosts = 678.63
tranType.closingCostsSeller = 325.65
tranType.discount = 0
tranType.land = 100000
tranType.loanAmount = 160000

# other credits create the classes
otherCreditType = OtherCreditType()

# other credits
otherCreditType.amount = 500.0
otherCreditType.description = "Realtors Fee"
```

```
# transaction type
tranType.otherCreditType = otherCreditType
tranType.pmi_MIP = 550.0
tranType.pmi_MIP_Financed = 550.0
tranType.prepaidItems = 1200.87
tranType.purchasePrice = 170000.0
tranType.refinance = 10000.0
tranType.subordinateFinancing = 0.0

# address type
currentAddress = AddressType()
currentAddress.addType = AddressEnum.CURRENT_ADDRESS
currentAddress.propertyType = propertyType
currentAddress.numberYears = 25
currentAddress.address_1 = "300 Redmond Avenue"
currentAddress.address_2 = ""
currentAddress.city = "Rockaway"
currentAddress.state = "NJ"
currentAddress.zipCode = "07866"

previousAddress = AddressType()
previousAddress.addType = AddressEnum.PREV_ADDRESS
# add the address to the addressList
# borrower type - primary borrower
mainBorrower = BorrowerType()
mainBorrower.address.append(currentAddress)
mainBorrower.address.append(previousAddress)

dateBirth = date(1963, 7, 12)
mainBorrower.dateOfBirth = dateBirth

# declarations
declarations = DeclarationsType()
declarations.anyJudgments = False
declarations.borrowedDownPayment = False
declarations.coMakerNote = False
```

```
declarations.declaredBankrupt = False
declarations.delinquent = False
declarations.lawsuit = False
declarations.obligatedOnAnyLoan = False
declarations.obligatedToPayAlimony = False
declarations.ownershipInterest = False
declarations.permanentResident = False
declarations.primaryResidence = False
declarations.propertyForeclosed = False
declarations.propertyType = PropertyTypeEnum.PRINCIPAL_RESIDENCE
mainBorrower.declarations = declarations

# dependents
dependents = Dependents()
dependents.name = "Mary Smith"
dependents.age = 55.6
mainBorrower.dependents.append(dependents)
# employment
employmentType = EmploymentType()
employer = Employer()
employer.name = "Blockchain Inc"
# employment address
employerAddress = AddressType()
employer.address.append(employerAddress)
employmentType.businessPhone = "8001230000"
employmentType.yearsInProfession = 20

# date time functions
dateTo = date.today()
dateFrom = date(2002, 1, 1)
employmentType.dateFrom = dateFrom
employmentType.dateTo = dateTo
employmentType.employer = employer
employmentType.isSelfEmployed = False
employmentType.monthlyIncome = 12000.0
employmentType.position = "Director"
```

```
employmentType.title = "Director"
employmentType.typeOfBusiness = "Software Development"
mainBorrower.employment = employmentType

# continuing with borrower type
mainBorrower.firstName = "Joe"
mainBorrower.lastName = "Smith"
mainBorrower.middleName = None
# Marital status
mainBorrower.borrower = BorrowerEnum.BORROWER
mainBorrower.maritalStatus = MaritalStatus.MARRIED
mainBorrower.setphone("9735122222")
mainBorrower.setssn("890867543")
mainBorrower.title = "Jr."
mainBorrower.yearsSchool = 22

# Income type
incomeType = IncomeType()
incomeType.baseEmployment = 200000.0
incomeType.bonuses = 12000.0
incomeType.commissions = 4000.0
incomeType.dividendsInterest = 575.0
incomeType.netRentalIncome = 10000.0
incomeType.other1 = 345.0
incomeType.other2 = 0.0

# Other income type
otherIncomeType = OtherIncomeType()
otherIncomeType.amount = 0.0
otherIncomeType.description = "None"
incomeType.otherIncome = otherIncomeType
incomeType.otherIncomeSources = 0.0
incomeType.overtime = 600.0
mainBorrower.income = incomeType
```

```
# government monitoring
governmentMonitoringType = GovernmentMonitoringType()
governmentMonitoringType.race = Ethnicity.WHITE
governmentMonitoringType.sex = Gender.MALE
mainBorrower.governmentMonitoring =
        governmentMonitoringType

# Second borrower or co-borrower
coBorrower = BorrowerType()
coBorrower.address.append(currentAddress)
dateBirth = date(1969, 11, 19)
coBorrower.dateOfBirth = dateBirth
coBorrower.declarations = declarations
coBorrower.dependents.append(dependents)
coBorrower.employment = EmploymentType()

# continuing with borrower type
coBorrower.firstName = "Jane"
coBorrower.lastName = "Smith"
coBorrower.middleName = "Diana"

# Marital status
coBorrower.Borrower = BorrowerEnum.CO_BORROWER
coBorrower.maritalStatus = MaritalStatus.MARRIED
coBorrower.setphone("9735122222")
coBorrower.setssn("890865123")
coBorrower.ssn1 = coBorrower.getssn(coBorrower.ssn)
coBorrower.title = ""
coBorrower.yearsSchool = 23
# government monitoring
gmt2 = GovernmentMonitoringType()
gmt2.race = Ethnicity.AFRICAN_AMERICAN
gmt2.sex = Gender.FEMALE
coBorrower.governmentMonitoring = gmt2

currentTime = date.today()
```

```
# main mortgage application
mortgageApp.agencyCaseNumber = "00137689"
mortgageApp.amortizationTypeDescription = "Mortgage"
mortgageApp.amount = 200000.56
mortgageApp.applicationID = "001"
mortgageApp.dateCreated = currentTime
mortgageApp.interestRate = 2.55
mortgageApp.lenderCaseNumber = "012356"
mortgageApp.numberOfMonths = 240
mortgageApp.otherIncomeIncluded = True
mortgageApp.otherLiabilitiesIncluded = True

# assign purpose
mortgageApp.purpose = purposeType
mortgageApp.representativeId = 12001
mortgageApp.sourceIdentifier = "1324"
# set the mortageapp to transaction type
mortgageApp.transactionType = tranType

mortgageApp.borrower = mainBorrower
mortgageApp.coborrower = coBorrower

# all assets and liabilities
al = AssetsLiabilities()

# alimony child support
alim = AlimonyChildSupport()
alim.monthlyPayment = 0
alim.monthsLeft = 0
alim.owedTo = 0
al.alimonyChildSupport = alim

# assets
assets = AssetType()
assets.amount = 12000
assets.description = "Life savings"
```

```
# checkings and savings
checkSavingsArrayList = []
checkSavings = CheckingSavingsAccount()
checkSavings.accountNumber = "10001001"
checkSavings.accountSequence = 1
checkSavingsAddress = AddressType()
checkSavingsAddress.address_1 = "101 Broadway"
checkSavingsAddress.address_2 = ""
checkSavingsAddress.city = "New York"
checkSavingsAddress.state = "NY"
checkSavingsAddress.zipCode = 10001
checkSavings.bankAddress = checkSavingsAddress
al.checkingsavings = checkSavings
checkSavingsArrayList.append(checkSavings)

# cash deposit
cashDepositArrayList = []
cashDepositType = CashDepositType()
cashDepositType.description="Deposit 1"
cashDepositType.amount = 10000
cashDepositArrayList.append(cashDepositType)
al.cashDeposit = cashDepositArrayList

# credit received
creditReceivedArray = []
creditReceived = CreditReceivedType()
creditReceived.accountNumber = "2000-3345-6666-7765"
creditReceived.alternateName = "Credit Card X"
creditReceived.creditorName = "Bank of Mars-Moon"
creditReceivedArray.append(creditReceived)
al.creditReceived = creditReceivedArray

# expense
expenseArrayList = []
expenseType = ExpenseType()
expenseType.firstMortgage = 1200.0
```

```
expenseType.hazardInsurance = 700
expenseType.homeownersAssnDues = 0
expenseType.mortgageInsurance = 300
expenseType.other = 0
expenseType.otherFinancing = 0
expenseType.realEstateTaxes = 450
expenseType.rent = 0
expenseArrayList.append(expenseType)
al.expense = expenseArrayList

# other income type
otherIncomeArrayList = []
otherIncomeTypeCommon = OtherIncomeType()
otherIncomeTypeCommon.description = "Other Income 1"
otherIncomeTypeCommon.amount = 1000

otherIncomeArrayList.append(otherIncomeTypeCommon)
al.otherIncome = otherIncomeArrayList

# job related expenses
jobRelatedExpList = []
jobRelatedExpense = JobRelatedExpenseType()
jobRelatedExpense.description = "Job Expenses 1"
jobRelatedExpense.monthlyPayment = 100
jobRelatedExpense.monthsLeft = 12
jobRelatedExpList.append(jobRelatedExpense)
al.jobExpenses = jobRelatedExpList

# Life insurance
lifeInsuranceList = []
li = LifeInsurance()
li.faceAmount = 1000.0
li.netCashvalue = 200000.0
lifeInsuranceList.append(li)
al.lifeInsurance = lifeInsuranceList
```

```
# Stocks and bonds
stockArrayList = []
stockBondsAccType = StocksBondsAccountType()
stockBondsAccType.accountSequence = 1
stockBondsAccType.amount = 20000.0
stockBondsAccType.description = "BLK Stocks"
stockArrayList.append(stockBondsAccType)
al.stocksBonds = stockArrayList
mortgageApp.assetsLiabilities = al
```

The remaining part of this service is in converting the mortgage application class into a serializable JSON and invoking the Hyperledger REST service running on a different server. This is a classic example of a machine to machine invocation through well-established APIs.

```
# return jsonpickle.encode(mortgageApp)
msgjson = mortgageApp.tojjson()
msg1 = mortgageApp.toJSON()
print (msg1)

fabric_cldata = {}
fabric_prdata = {}
url = "http://localhost:3000/api/"
urlclt = url + "Client"
urlprt = url + "Portfolio"
```

The method below creates a new client using the REST server running Composer and Fabric. The client id is the agency case number concatenated with a random number to bring in uniqueness.

```
fabric_cldata['$class'] = 'com.devb.consolidated.Client'
clid = mortgageApp.agencyCaseNumber
      + str(random.randint(1,21)*5)
fabric_cldata['clientId'] = clid
fabric_cldata['name'] = mainBorrower.firstName + ' ' +
      mainBorrower.lastName
self.postFabric(urlclt, fabric_cldata)
```

The method outlined below creates the portfolio where the lending structured as a JSON object can be stored as a transaction.

```
fabric_prdata['$class'] = 'com.devb.consolidated.Portfolio'
fabric_prdata['portfolioId']=mortgageApp.lenderCaseNumber
      + str(random.randint(1,21)*5)
fabric_prdata['client'] = 'com.devb.consolidated.Client#' +clid
fabric_prdata['value'] = tranType.loanAmount
fabric_prdata['jsonAsset'] = msg1
self.postFabric(urlprt, fabric_prdata)
return (msgjson)

def postFabric(self, turl, tjson):
  request = urllib.request.Request(turl)
  # add appropriate header
  request.add_header('Content-Type','application/json;
        charset=utf-8')
  jsonSentData = json.dumps(tjson)
  jsonSentAsBytes = jsonSentData.encode('utf-8')
```

```
        request.add_header('Content-Length', len(jsonSentAsBytes))
        print(jsonSentAsBytes)
        response = urllib.request.urlopen(request, jsonSentAsBytes)
        return response

@app.errorhandler(404)
def server_error(e):
    # Log the error
    logging.exception('An error occurred during a request.')
    return 'Mortgage URL Application: An internal error occurred.', 404
api.add_resource(UrlaService, '/mortgage/webapi/urla/<string:appid>')

if __name__ == '__main__':
    app.run(debug=True)
```

Defined in the technology textbooks, transferring assets is the core functionality of a blockchain. How people buy, sell or barter goods in a business network with no governing body or policy makes blockchain an invaluable power-tool. Mortgage, be it conventional or unconventional loan is a party to such transfers of assets. In the exceedingly regulated world of banking, blockchain provides a different flavor of such transfers, much different from the present.

Hyperledger Fabric or Sawtooth as the blockchain of choice offer a strong separation of concerns. Separation of concerns (SoC) is a design principle for separating a computer program into distinct sections, such that each section addresses a separate concern. A concern is a set of information that affects the code of a computer program.

- Business application (the source of engagement)
- Hyperledger composer or Seth (the digitization of resources, roles, functions, events and transactions)
- Hyperledger fabric, sawtooth or blockchain – the systems integration, the source of truth

For those who read my earlier articles on V-Design can well correlate the Vs, Vr and Vt aspects of the design. The above structure also lends itself to what a typical consulting engagement in blockchain would entail. I spent some time with small to medium sized banks educating them on the features, besides how blockchain could lower closing costs and complete a standard loan underwriting in minutes. An engagement model emerged from such discussions that I will share with you. Solutions around distributed ledgers go beyond the proofs – of concepts and technologies to how they can be shrink-wrapped into a profitable engagement.

Exploratory phase
Between you and the business, this phase is the first one to engage in. Discuss and agree on the Blockchain, its definitions and applicability. Blockchain is not one size that fits all. There may not be any need for blockchain, for all you know. In the mortgage scenario, you can apply an 80-20 rule that promises success in most cases.

Digitization phase

As the exploratory phase progresses into more meaningful discussions, it gives you the opportunity to define and design the structure, network, participants, assets, roles, transactions, events and policies. This is about the White-board, White-board and the White-board. You may do it on a slate, with dry markers or whatever comes in handy, but someone needs to complete it with a passion.

Disruption phase

Once you arrive at an agreement, there comes the time to explore the functions. Iterate and build. This is one phase where short sleeved tee-shirts and jugs of coffee are indispensable.

Scale and deploy

Re-engineer, refactor and integrate. A self-explanatory segment, it's the least abstract, and highly focused phase.

The Hyperledger construct of a model is analogous to a model in UML. Designed are static and structural models to portray participants, assets, transaction and events. Transactions and events get expressed through the behavioral scripts. Digitization of access rules and other policies become a part of the access control files. A distinct *"namespace"* sets the business-network apart from the rest. Yes, Hyperledger composer lets the parties define their *"business network"*, a carefully chosen gathering of people and machines who have in common a specific contract. The business network owes its definition to the artifacts and rules which get compiled and digitized for different deployment environments.

Several participants access the "business network" where they may even undertake to maintain it. The maintainer of the network runs many hardware "peer nodes", sustaining the system. To prevent a crash, Hyperledger fabric replicates the distributed ledger across such peer nodes.

Composer modeling language expresses the domain model of the business network. The model, once constructed, allows developers to capture "smart contracts" as '*executable transaction processor functions*', written in JavaScript. In both Hyperledger Fabric and Sawtooth, the construct is semantically JavaScript.

In a nutshell, a good knowledge of UML helps in writing the models and contracts in the different blockchain modeling language and knowing server-side JavaScript, Python or Go helps define the scripts that express the structure of the transactions. Mocha and Chai are invaluable in testing against the Node.JS embedded engine. Microsoft's VS-Code is another invaluable editor and lint tool in managing all that parsing and syntax. In both Fabric and Sawtooth-Seth, you end up defining:

- The Network
- The Smart Contract, its structure and behavior
- Rules of access
- Query and reporting (optional)

Let us try our hand at the consolidated-network that brings the two financial services to an interconnected-mix serving the last exercise in this book. This solution implemented in Fabric is accessible to the Python middleware code.

Start Fabric and run the Yeoman CLI command to initialize the network. The sequence of commands that follow are without any description as I felt it would be an unnecessary repetition.

```
$ export FABRIC_VERSION=hlfv11
$ rm -fr ~/.composer
$ ./startFabric.sh
$ ./createPeerAdminCard.sh
$ yo hyperledger-composer:businessnetwork
```

```
Welcome to the business network generator
? Business network name: consolidated-network
? Description: Complete Financial Planning and Loans
? Author name:  DevB
? Author email: devb@linux.com
? License: Apache-2.0
? Namespace: com.devb.consolidated
   create package.json
   ...
```

```
$ cd consolidated-network/
```

```
$ composer archive create -t dir -n .
```

```
Creating Business Network Archive
Looking for package.json of Business Network
Definition
        Input directory: /home/devb/my-
network/fabric-tools/consolidated-network
Found:
        Description: Complete Financial Planning and
Loans
        Name: consolidated-network
        Identifier: consolidated-network@0.0.1
Written Business Network Definition Archive file to
        Output file: consolidated-network@0.0.1.bna
Command succeeded
```

$ composer network install --archiveFile consolidated-network@0.0.1.bna --card PeerAdmin@hlfv1

```
✔ Installing business network. This may take a
minute...
Successfully installed business network consolidated-
network, version 0.0.1
Command succeeded
```

$ composer network start --networkName consolidated-network --networkVersion 0.0.1 --card PeerAdmin@hlfv1 --networkAdmin admin --networkAdminEnrollSecret adminpw

```
Starting business network consolidated-network at
version 0.0.1
Processing these Network Admins:
      userName: admin
✔ Starting business network definition. This may
take a minute...
Successfully created business network card:
      Filename: admin@consolidated-network.card
Command succeeded
```

$ composer card import --file admin@consolidated-network.card

```
Successfully imported business network card
      Card file: admin@consolidated-network.card
      Card name: admin@consolidated-network
Command succeeded
```

$ composer-rest-server

```
? Enter the name of the business network card to use:
admin@consolidated-network
? Specify if you want namespaces in the generated
REST API: never use namespaces
? Specify if you want to enable authentication for
the REST API using Passport: No
? Specify if you want to enable event publication
over WebSockets: No
? Specify if you want to enable TLS security for the
REST API: No
To restart the REST server using the same options,
issue the following command:
    composer-rest-server -c admin@consolidated-network
-n never
Discovering types from business network definition
```

```
...
Discovered types from business network definition
Generating schemas for all types in business network
definition ...
Generated schemas for all types in business network
definition
Adding schemas for all types to Loopback ...
Added schemas for all types to Loopback
Web server listening at: http://localhost:3000
Browse your REST API at
http://localhost:3000/explorer
```

The Python client *'consolidated_client.py'* built earlier, can now invoke the contract and send the entire URLA-JSON as a transaction to the Fabric blockchain setup. It is also possible to do the same through the user-interface built during the code generation.

Scaling, Provisioning and Building the Peer Network

While it's easy to start something locally and complete the design successfully on your laptop, it remains a big task to scale the application to a real-life peer-to-peer network. I will design a topography with two or more servers running in the cloud that mimic the peer-nodes. For our servers, I will provision two instances of AWS EC2 t2-medium equipped with Ubuntu 16.0.4, 4 GB RAM and 8 GB SSD. Think of these two instances ec2-52-91-186-129.compute-1.amazonaws.com and ec2-54-227-87-243.compute-1.amazonaws.com as peers in the Sawtooth business network.

Figure 35 - AWS EC2 Console

We will setup one instance and use its Snapshot to recreate the other. To enable the chatter that needs to happen between the peer nodes, we open a few ports on the firewall. Though I have kept them open to the world, you can restrict their communication to just the server IP-addresses. Setting up a tight security group for the instances comes next on the task list.

Custom TCP Rule	TCP	8080	xxx.xxx.xxx.xxx/32
Custom TCP Rule	TCP	4004	0.0.0.0/0
SSH	TCP	22	xxx.xxx.xxx.xxx/32
Custom TCP Rule	TCP	8800	0.0.0.0/0
Custom TCP Rule	TCP	8008	0.0.0.0/0
Custom TCP Rule	TCP	3030	0.0.0.0/0

We will also assign key-pairs to the EC2-instances. You can create a new key-pair – 'provblock.pem'. You must confirm that the public key is changed to read-only and secure before running the secured shell command.

```
$ chmod 400 ~provblock.pem
$ ssh -i ~provblock.pem ubuntu@ec2-52-91-186-129.compute-
1.amazonaws.com
```

This will all you to access the remote instance running on AWS.

```
$ git clone https://github.com/hyperledger/sawtooth-seth
cd sawtooth-seth/
$ sudo apt-get update
$ sudo apt-get install apt-transport-https ca-certificates curl
software-properties-common

$ curl -fsSL https://download.docker.com/linux/ubuntu/gpg | sudo
apt-key add -

$ sudo add-apt-repository "deb [arch=amd64]
https://download.docker.com/linux/ubuntu $(lsb_release -cs)
stable"

$ sudo apt-get update
$ sudo apt-get install docker-ce
$ sudo curl -L
https://github.com/docker/compose/releases/download/1.20.1/doc
ker-compose-`uname -s`-`uname -m` -o /usr/local/bin/docker-
compose

$ sudo chmod +x /usr/local/bin/docker-compose
docker-compose --version
```

```
$ sudo docker-compose up --build
```

Open another terminal window and access the same server.

```
$ ssh -i ~provblock.pem ubuntu@ec2-52-91-186-129.compute-1.amazonaws.com
$ sudo docker ps
// Now shell into the seth-rpc container
$ sudo docker exec -it seth-rpc bash
```

Within the container -
example - root@38a8e7f51187:/project/sawtooth-seth/rpc#

```
$ npm install -g solc
$ apt-get update
$ apt-get install nano
$ openssl ecparam -genkey -name secp256k1 | openssl ec -out alias.pem -aes128
$ seth account import alias.pem myalias
$ seth account create --nonce=0 --wait myalias
```

```
Account created
Transaction Receipt: {
  "TransactionID":
"f08c188f60804d731832fdd802e742cd99f27020da057ed0f022613b598
6c9be4621ceea028d65eade0d68de6e18cc0e4baa381a9faac7dd7609b9
b6ffaf4243",
  "Address": "45e4c1233ce2e952eb159e7d4109f88a5aae6a4a"
}
```

```
$ cp alias.pem /root/.sawtooth/
$ seth init http://rest-api:8008
$ seth-rpc --connect tcp://comp-seth-rpc:4004 --bind 0.0.0.0:3030
--unlock alias
```

Check out the peers, if they are accessible.

http://ec2-52-91-186-129.compute-1.amazonaws.com:8008/peers
http://ec2-54-227-87-243.compute-1.amazonaws.com:8008/peers

Re-run the validator if necessary.

```
sawtooth-validator -vv --endpoint tcp://validator:8800 --bind
component:tcp://eth0:4004 --bind network:tcp://eth0:8800
```

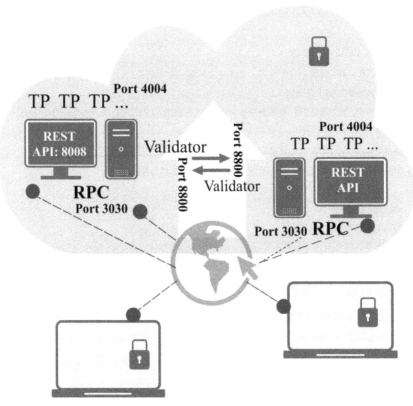

Figure 36 - Sawtooth Seth Network Configuration

 Running the contracts does not change. Just use one server to run the Seth-CLI. Each host system, whether a physical computer, virtual machine, or set of Docker containers must run at least one validator, an optional REST API, and an identical set of transaction processors. Sawtooth run-time environment must include the Sawtooth REST API and SETH-RPC on all validator nodes. Each validator node publicizes a routable address and Docker platform provides a preconfigured setting. Authorization-type stays the same with all nodes, either using a trust or a challenge mechanism. The genesis block gets created for the first validator node only, including on-chain configuration settings, such as the consensus-type, that becomes available to the new validator nodes joining the network. Keeping the port 8800 open helps the validators to communicate among themselves.

While several distinct architectures, user stories and code on financial planning, real estate and mortgage have taken the center-stage, I reckon few things may have gone awry. While preparing the manuscript, I encountered many choices that confronted me and I tried to write them all. Without sounding any more defensive, I admit, there were many occasions where newer technologies overlaid with older property listings, search queries and loan parameters may had confused you the reader. But, from the content point of view, all the architecture and patterns must have served their purpose. From a continuity point of view, the transitions may have been rough. As always, I solicit your feedback on areas the book can undergo improvement. Github.com/devbnj is the best place to leave your feedback and download a copy of the code.

RUNNING FABRIC 1.2+ IN THE CLOUD

One of the big challenges a developer or an operator is likely to face with Hyperledger Fabric 1.3 or its latest version is how he can move from a sandbox to a true production environment. Like most Hyperledger fans, I faced similar hassles running in a production environment. I loved that Alibaba Cloud offers a barebones Ubuntu 16.0.4 64-bit no-frills environment at an unbeatable price which I can safely assume as production.

Now as I write, Alibaba Cloud Elastic Computing Instance of 2 VCPU, 4 GB RAM and 40 GB diskspace comes unbridled. You have complete control over it, which is useful, yet brings other security issues.

There are three resources you will use while interacting with a cloud instance.

The Instance itself – which is easier managed through the console. I will refer this to as 'console'

The application running on the EC Instance – In our case it is Hyperledger Fabric – Latest version. I refer this as the 'instance' in the document.

The Local machine through which you access the instance. I refer this to as 'local' in the document.

CONSOLE: One of the first things you do is define a security group that goes with the instance. Hyperledger Fabric is a bunch of applications that comprises the Blockchain, Kafka, Zookeeper and CouchDB database. Which means clearly that we will keep certain ports open as the network scales and accommodates more peers. Defining the port ranges may result in external communication. It requires port 22 for SSH, 80 preferably is great for HTTP and 443 for HTTPS. Additionally, you may want to open ports that may require you to communicate with CouchDB or ports that Kafka and Zookeeper.

CONSOLE: The next thing you do is to change the password. The EC instance comes with a default password which is great as it is hard to remember and even harder to crack. But I find it easier to set the instance with a password I can remember.

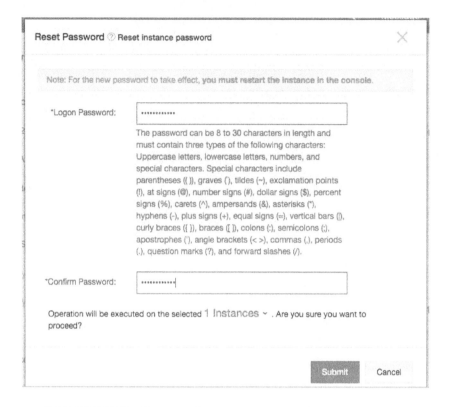

CONSOLE: Remember to restart the server instance after making these changes.

CONSOLE: The next thing you do in the console is create a certificate (keys) that you can use to SSH or Telnet into the server instance. Create the SSH keys and set its binding to the server. In our case, we created *"alikeys.pem"* for download and use in SSH.

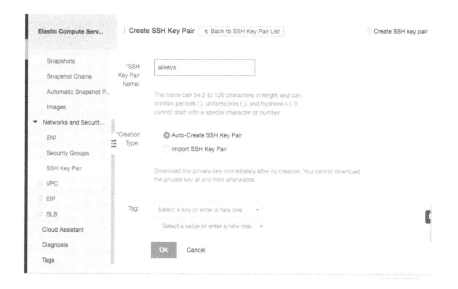

CONSOLE: Once you have generated the certificates, bind these keys to the server instance. This will ensure your ability to use a local instance to log into the server with these keys. In case you have re-initialized the server, which I have done often, it will be a good idea to re-run the local instance to adapt to the new SSH server environment.

LOCAL: In this case, you would run:

```
$ ssh-keygen -R [xx.xx.xxx.xxx]
# - your server IP address
```

CONSOLE: The console gives you an option in generating keys or using an existing key for different instances. The "bind" and "unbind" options allow the certificate keys to be either bound or unbound to an instance.

LOCAL: Download the keys to your local machine and convert the keys to read-only before using with SSH.

```
$ chmod 400 alikeys.pem
```

CONSOLE: Just a quick recap. So far, on your console, you reset the password. Generated the keys and bound them to the server instance. Your names and keys may follow a different nomenclature from the name shown. Allow me to put on my architecture hat on naming conventions. In the cloud, often the instances grow into a large number. Naming them properly will give you the ability to rapidly search and monitor an instance. The naming convention used here is far from it, but having cloud instances for development, staging and production gives you an idea of how you want to qualify the instance naming.

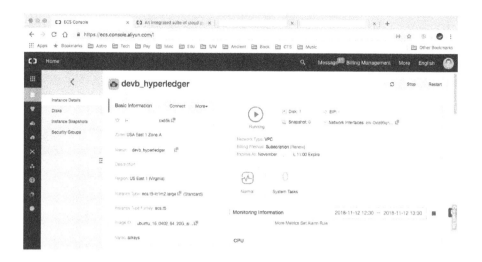

LOCAL: Now from your local machine, SSH into the server instance.

```
$ ssh -i ~/nodejs/alikeys.pem root@xx.xx.xxx.1xx
Welcome to Ubuntu 16.04.4 LTS (GNU/Linux 4.4.0-117-
generic x86_64)
 * Documentation:  https://help.ubuntu.com
 * Management:     https://landscape.canonical.com
 * Support:        https://ubuntu.com/advantage
Welcome to Alibaba Cloud Elastic Compute Service !
```

INSTANCE: Working as ROOT is not preferred from a security point of view either in development or production. It is time to create a new user, devb (*or your user name*) and assign it to the SUDO group.

```
$ adduser devb
$ usermod -aG sudo devb
$ su - devb
```

INSTANCE: Next, we install Fabric 1.3 prerequisites as the new user.

```
$ cd ~
$ curl -O
https://hyperledger.github.io/composer/v0.19/prereqs-
ubuntu.sh
```

```
$ chmod u+x prereqs-ubuntu.sh
$ ./prereqs-ubuntu.sh
```

-- it will install the following

Node: v8.12.0

npm: 6.4.1

Docker: Docker version 18.09.0, build 4d60db4

Docker Compose: docker-compose version 1.13.0, build 1719ceb

Python: Python 2.7.12

INSTANCE: Check the node.js and docker version and reboot.

```
$ node -v
$ reboot
```

LOCAL: At the reboot, your SSH session ends. You will have to re-SSH into the server instance to continue the installation.

```
$ ssh -i ~/nodejs/alikeys.pem root@xx.xx.xxx.xxx
$ su - devb
```

INSTANCE: The package add-apt-repository is likely not installed on your system. But if you try to use sudo apt-get install add-apt-repository, it won't work. Install the software properties to keep going.

```
$ sudo apt-get install software-properties-common
```

INSTANCE: Download the Fabric 1.3 meant for the cloud that I have configured using Yeasy and Fabric-Samples from Hyperledger Fabric.

```
$ mkdir {install-dir} && cd {install-dir}
$ curl -LkSs
https://api.github.com/repos/devbnj/fabric-
cloud/tarball -o fabric-cloud.tar.gz
$ tar -xvf fabric-cloud.tar.gz
```

INSTANCE: You may need Go-lang, if you want to add Smart Contracts or ChainCode.

```
$ sudo apt-get update
$ sudo apt-get -y upgrade
$ curl -O
https://storage.googleapis.com/golang/go1.11.2.linux-
amd64.tar.gz
$ sudo mv go /usr/local
$ sudo nano ~/.profile
```

```
# -- add to the end
export GOROOT=$HOME/go
export GOPATH=$HOME/work
export PATH=$PATH:$GOROOT/bin:$GOPATH/bin
export
FABRIC_CFG_PATH=/home/{user}/{install}/hyperledger_fabric/roo
t/config
# -- added
$ source ~/.profile
# -- test go
$ go version
```

INSTANCE: Now install Fabric 1.3 on docker containers and the samples.

```
$ curl -sSL http://bit.ly/2ysbOFE | bash -s 1.2.1
$ export PATH=/home/devb/bin:$PATH
```

INSTANCE: One thing you will notice in the samples is they offer examples from basic to advanced. Let's run the first network and more complex scenarios.

```
$ cd ~/{install directory}/hyperledger_fabric/fabric-
samples/scripts
$ ./bootstrap.sh
# -- this will install the binaries and docker images
```

```
Installing Hyperledger Fabric binaries
===> Downloading: …
Installing Hyperledger Fabric docker images
===> Pulling fabric Images
…
```

```
# -- now we move to the first network
$ cd ~/{install dir}/hyperledger_fabric/fabric-
samples/first-network
# -- generate the certificates and keys
$ ./byfn.sh generate
# -- start the containers for node.js and keep the
local database as couch-db
$ ./byfn.sh up -l node -s couchdb
```

…
/home/{user}/{install}/hyperledger_fabric/fabric-samples/first-network/../bin/cryptogen
###
Generate certificates using cryptogen tool
###
++ cryptogen generate --config=./crypto-config.yaml
org1.example.com
org2.example.com
++ res=0
++ set +x
/home/{user}/{install}/hyperledger_fabric/fabric-samples/first-network/../bin/configtxgen
###
######### Generating Orderer Genesis block #############
###
++ configtxgen -profile TwoOrgsOrdererGenesis -outputBlock ./channel-artifacts/genesis.block
…
###
Generating channel configuration transaction 'channel.tx'
###
++ configtxgen -profile TwoOrgsChannel -outputCreateChannelTx ./channel-artifacts/channel.tx -channelID mychannel
###

```
#######   Generating anchor peer update for Org1MSP  ##########
#################################################################
++ configtxgen -profile TwoOrgsChannel -
outputAnchorPeersUpdate ./channel-artifacts/Org1MSPanchors.tx
-channelID mychannel -asOrg Org1MSP
...
Creating network "net_byfn" with the default driver
Creating volume "..."
Creating cli ... done
Build your first network (BYFN) end-to-end test
Channel name : mychannel
Creating channel...
# -- have all peers join the channel created
Having all peers join the channel...
+ peer channel join -b mychannel.block
# -- install the Chaincode on different peers
Install chaincode on peer0.org2...
+ peer chaincode install -n mycc -v 1.0 -l node -p
/opt/gopath/src/github.com/chaincode/chaincode_example02/node
/
# -- instantiate the Chaincode
Instantiating chaincode on peer0.org2...
# -- query the Chaincode
Querying chaincode on peer0.org1...
+ peer chaincode query -C mychannel -n mycc -c
'{"Args":["query","a"]}'
Attempting to Query peer0.org1 ...3 secs
========= All GOOD, BYFN execution completed ===========
```

INSTANCE: Let's check the state of the containers. "docker ps" will show the results. A lot of containers have been used and testes against. There are three instances of couchdb, 2 peers and two organizations, the cli and others managed by docker.

```
devb@devb-hyperledger:~/devbhj2/devbhj-fabric-cloud-60a556d/hyperledger_fabric/fabric-samples/first-network$ docker ps
CONTAINER ID    IMAGE                                                                                        COMMAND              CREATED          ST
ATUS            PORTS                                                        NAMES
0c677279ca80    dev-peer1.org2.example.com-mycc-1.0-26c2ef32939554aac4f7ad6f100aca065e87959c9a126e06d764c8d01f8346eb   "/bin/sh -c 'cd /usr..."   16 minutes ago   Up
16 minutes                                                                   dev-peer1.org2.example.com-mycc-1.0
7a1c57fd1f6b    dev-peer0.org1.example.com-mycc-1.0-384f11f484b9302df90b453200cfb2517f43b05fce8f53f4e94d45ee3b6cab8ce9   "/bin/sh -c 'cd /usr..."   17 minutes ago   Up
17 minutes                                                                   dev-peer0.org1.example.com-mycc-1.0
4b44d499e12b    dev-peer0.org2.example.com-mycc-1.0-15b571b3ce849066b7ec74497da3b27e54e0df1345daf73951b94245ce00c42b   "/bin/sh -c 'cd /usr..."   17 minutes ago   Up
17 minutes                                                                   dev-peer0.org2.example.com-mycc-1.0
e429bfbfe971    hyperledger/fabric-tools:latest                              cli                          "/bin/bash"          18 minutes ago   Up
18 minutes
2e02bcfc6892    hyperledger/fabric-peer:latest                               peer0.org1.example.com       "peer node start"    18 minutes ago   Up
18 minutes      0.0.0.0:7051->7051/tcp, 0.0.0.0:7053->7053/tcp
4eef04832b23    hyperledger/fabric-peer:latest                               peer1.org1.example.com       "peer node start"    18 minutes ago   Up
18 minutes      0.0.0.0:8051->7051/tcp, 0.0.0.0:8053->7053/tcp
a4803f04dda2    hyperledger/fabric-peer:latest                               peer1.org2.example.com       "peer node start"    18 minutes ago   Up
18 minutes      0.0.0.0:10051->7051/tcp, 0.0.0.0:10053->7053/tcp
9ce3b4528e0e    hyperledger/fabric-peer:latest                               peer0.org2.example.com       "peer node start"    18 minutes ago   Up
18 minutes      0.0.0.0:9051->7051/tcp, 0.0.0.0:9053->7053/tcp
4632cb3bf4ae    hyperledger/fabric-couchdb                                   couchdb0                     "tini -- /docker-ent..."   18 minutes ago   Up
18 minutes      4369/tcp, 9100/tcp, 0.0.0.0:5984->5984/tcp
749c54d2868    hyperledger/fabric-orderer:latest                            orderer.example.com          "orderer"            18 minutes ago   Up
18 minutes      0.0.0.0:7050->7050/tcp
2b512d4921ba    hyperledger/fabric-couchdb                                   couchdb3                     "tini -- /docker-ent..."   18 minutes ago   Up
18 minutes      4369/tcp, 9100/tcp, 0.0.0.0:8984->5984/tcp
3dfcb495b0fc    hyperledger/fabric-couchdb                                   couchdb2                     "tini -- /docker-ent..."   18 minutes ago   Up
18 minutes      4369/tcp, 9100/tcp, 0.0.0.0:7984->5984/tcp
5cf3e8ab6bd7    hyperledger/fabric-couchdb                                   couchdb1                     "tini -- /docker-ent..."   18 minutes ago   Up
18 minutes      4369/tcp, 9100/tcp, 0.0.0.0:6984->5984/tcp
```

INSTANCE: Let's try a few scenarios with the YEASY or Baohua Yang's configuration. He has some tests that are in the same download. The tests are similar with 2 orgs and 4 peers.

```
$ RELEASE=v1.3.0
$ cd ${RELEASE};
$ make setup download
$ make start
```

Start a fabric network with docker-compose-2orgs-4peers-solo.yaml...

make[1]: Entering directory '/home/{user}/{install}/fabric-cloud/hyperledger_fabric/v1.3.0'

Clean all HLF containers and chaincode images

…

May manually clean the crypto-config, solo/channel-artifacts and org3/crypto-config

make[1]: Leaving directory '/home/{user}/{install}/fabric-cloud/hyperledger_fabric/v1.3.0'

Pulling cli (yeasy/hyperledger-fabric:1.3.0)...

…

$ make test

Create channel on the fabric network

=== Creating channel businesschannel with businesschannel.tx... ===

=== Create Channel businesschannel by org 1/peer 0 ===

=== Channel businesschannel is created. ===

=== Created channel businesschannel with businesschannel.tx ===

…

Join channel

=== Join peers 0 from org 1 into businesschannel... ===

=== Join org 1/peer 0 into channel businesschannel ===
=== org 1/peer 0 joined into channel businesschannel ===
=== Join org 1/peer 1 into channel businesschannel ===
=== org 1/peer 1 joined into channel businesschannel ===
=== Join org 2/peer 0 into channel businesschannel ===
=== org 2/peer 0 joined into channel businesschannel ===
=== Join org 2/peer 1 into channel businesschannel ===
=== org 2/peer 1 joined into channel businesschannel ===
=== Join peers 0 from org 1 into businesschannel Complete ===

List the joined channels

=== Listing joined channels... ===
=== List the channels that org1/peer0 joined ===
=== Done to list the channels that org1/peer0 joined ===
=== List the channels that org1/peer1 joined ===
=== Done to list the channels that org1/peer1 joined ===
=== List the channels that org2/peer0 joined ===
=== Done to list the channels that org2/peer0 joined ===
=== List the channels that org2/peer1 joined ===
=== Done to list the channels that org2/peer1 joined ===
=== Done listing joined channels ===

Get info of the app channel

=== Getting info of channel businesschannel... ===
=== Get channel info of businesschannel with id of org1/peer0 ===
=== Done to get channel info of businesschannel with id of org1/peer0 ===
=== Get channel info of businesschannel with id of org1/peer1 ===
=== Done to get channel info of businesschannel with id of org1/peer1 ===
=== Get channel info of businesschannel with id of org2/peer0 ===
=== Done to get channel info of businesschannel with id of org2/peer0 ===
=== Get channel info of businesschannel with id of org2/peer1 ===
=== Done to get channel info of businesschannel with id of org2/peer1 ===
=== Get info of channel businesschannel Complete ===

make[2]: Leaving directory '/home/{user}/{install}/hyperledger_fabric/v1.3.0'
make update_anchors

make[2]: Entering directory
'/home/{user}/{install}/hyperledger_fabric/v1.3.0'
Update anchors on the fabric network
=== Updating anchor peers to peer0 for org1... ===
=== Update config on channel businesschannel ===
=== Channel businesschannel is updated. ===

```
=== Updating anchor peers to peer0 for org2... ===
=== Update config on channel businesschannel ===
=== Channel businesschannel is updated. ===
=== Updated anchor peers ===

...

...
```

INSTANCE: The docker ps command shows the different containers managed through Docker.

```
devb@devb-hyperledger:~/devbmj/fabric-cloud/hyperledger_fabric/v1.3.0$ docker ps
CONTAINER ID   IMAGE                                          COMMAND              CREATED        S
TATUS          PORTS                                                               NAMES
44113f587c97   dev-peer1.org2.example.com-exp02-1.0-ac79f954aa10befb402e8d87d56741bcfae7738c8fd82aee62f22874f759e30d   "chaincode -peer.add…"   7 minutes ago    U
p 7 minutes                                                                         dev-peer1.org2.example.com-exp02-1.0
73d726ab4a34   dev-peer0.org1.example.com-exp02-1.0-207541cceae707183f8108fcfc8ad03b450411570fb69827d3d40dc2ffdddbb4   "chaincode -peer.add…"   7 minutes ago    U
p 7 minutes                                                                         dev-peer0.org1.example.com-exp02-1.0
3fef34f2f64f   yeasy/hyperledger-fabric-peer:1.3.0                                  "peer node start"     8 minutes ago    U
p 8 minutes    0.0.0.0:8051->7051/tcp, 0.0.0.0:8052->7052/tcp, 0.0.0.0:8053->7053/tcp   peer1.org1.example.com
88b833ca5e72   yeasy/hyperledger-fabric-peer:1.3.0                                  "peer node start"     8 minutes ago    U
p 8 minutes    0.0.0.0:7051->7051/tcp                                               peer0.org1.example.com
84d33c9f687c   yeasy/hyperledger-fabric-peer:1.3.0                                  "peer node start"     8 minutes ago    U
p 8 minutes    0.0.0.0:9051->7051/tcp, 0.0.0.0:9052->7052/tcp, 0.0.0.0:9053->7053/tcp   peer0.org2.example.com
72ee8c487e9e   yeasy/hyperledger-fabric-peer:1.3.0                                  "peer node start"     8 minutes ago    U
p 8 minutes    0.0.0.0:10051->7051/tcp, 0.0.0.0:10052->7052/tcp, 0.0.0.0:10053->7053/tcp   peer1.org2.example.com
cce0d11d66ba   yeasy/hyperledger-fabric-orderer:1.3.0                               "orderer start"       8 minutes ago    U
p 8 minutes    0.0.0.0:7050->7050/tcp                                               orderer0.example.com
7f877e9a115f   yeasy/hyperledger-fabric:1.3.0                                       "bash -c 'cd /tmp; s…"   8 minutes ago    U
p 8 minutes    7050-7054/tcp                                                        fabric-cli
```

```
$ make stop
# -- this will stop all the containers
```

INSTANCE: It's time to test the blockchain setup from a remote client.

INSTANCE: Let's now install Hyperledger Fabric Composer latest from the Github server. Install Hyperledger Composer 0.20 CLI SDK along with it. This step may be unwanted if you plan to use Go-lang to create ChainCode and use the SDK with languages like Java, Python or NodeJS. To maintain a common language of communication, most of the commands in this article are JavaScript based. Also, after you have logged in, change over as the Sudo User when you have SSH'd into the server.

```
$ npm install -g composer-rest-server@0.20
$ npm install -g composer-cli@0.20
$ npm install -g generator-hyperledger-composer@0.20
$ npm install -g yo
```

```
$ npm install -g composer-playground@0.20
# -- this will stop all the containers
$ docker kill $(docker ps -q)
$ docker rm $(docker ps -a -q)
```

```
$ cd ~/{install}/hyperledger_fabric/fabric-dev-
servers/
$ export FABRIC_VERSION=hlfv12
$ ./ startFabric.sh
```

This will start the Hyperledger Fabric 1.2 or 1.3 instance with a few peers.

```
$ ./createPeerAdminCard.sh
```
Development only script for Hyperledger Fabric control
Running 'createPeerAdminCard.sh'
FABRIC_VERSION is set to 'hlfv12'
FABRIC_START_TIMEOUT is unset, assuming 15 (seconds)
Using composer-cli at v0.20.4
Successfully created business network card file to
      Output file: /tmp/PeerAdmin@hlfv1.card
Command succeeded
Successfully imported business network card
      Card file: /tmp/PeerAdmin@hlfv1.card
      Card name: PeerAdmin@hlfv1
Command succeeded
Hyperledger Composer PeerAdmin card has been imported, host
of fabric specified as 'localhost'

```
$ yo hyperledger-composer:businessnetwork
```
We're constantly looking for ways to make yo better!
May we anonymously report usage statistics to improve the tool
over time?
More info: https://github.com/yeoman/insight & http://yeoman.io
$ No
Welcome to the business network generator
? Business network name: health-plan

? Description: health plan
? Author name: devb
? Author email: devb@linux.com
? License: Apache-2.0
? Namespace: com.devb.health
? Do you want to generate an empty template network? No:
generate a populated sample network
   create package.json
   create README.md
   create models/com.devb.health.cto
   create permissions.acl
   create .eslintrc.yml
   create features/sample.feature
   create features/support/index.js
   create test/logic.js
   create lib/logic.js

$ cd health-plan
$ composer archive create -t dir -n .
$ composer network install --card PeerAdmin@hlfv1 --archiveFile
health-plan@0.0.1.bna

```
$ composer network start --networkName health-plan --
networkVersion 0.0.1 --networkAdmin admin --
networkAdminEnrollSecret adminpw --card
PeerAdmin@hlfv1 --file healthplan.card
$ composer card import --file healthplan.card
$ composer network ping --card admin@health-plan
$ composer-rest-server
```

? Enter the name of the business network card to use:
admin@health-plan
? Specify if you want namespaces in the generated REST API:
never use namespaces
? Specify if you want to use an API key to secure the REST API:
No
? Specify if you want to enable authentication for the REST API
using Passport: No
? Specify if you want to enable the explorer test interface: Yes

? Specify a key if you want to enable dynamic logging: no
? Specify if you want to enable event publication over WebSockets: No
? Specify if you want to enable TLS security for the REST API: No
To restart the REST server using the same options, issue the following command:

```
composer-rest-server -c admin@health-plan -n never -u true -d n
```

CONSOLE: Ensure port 3000 is open in the security group that connects to this instance. It is important this issue be resolved at its inception. Port 80 and 443 may be closed, unless the Node.JS code acts simply as a delegate.

CONSOLE: If port 3000 is unopened, then one can add a new rule that ensures the port is open to HTTP or TCP communications. At this juncture it is also a good idea to check the IP address that is exposed to Internet, not private. Which implies, all communication to the RESTful interface that you are about to expose will be the internet address: 3000.

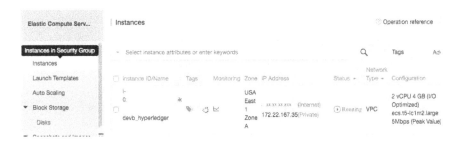

LOCAL: Open your web browser and type http://[above internet IP address]:3000 and you can view the web application that exposes the blockchain application to accept transactions, add participants and others.

This opens a new world onto the distributed systems environment. Blockchain systems such as Hyperledger Fabric are mostly machine-to-machine communication. The only intervention comes from introducing a new private network, or adding participants or adding or modifying a smart contract in other words the underlying Chaincode. The ability to interact smart with a set of peers, orderers, Chaincode and CLIs becomes the business case for the next-gen computing standards.

***

RUNNING SAWTOOTH 1.0.5 ON THE CLOUD.

Sawtooth as we know by now, is another powerful Permissioned Blockchain Network offering from Hyperledger. Intel Corp. drives Sawtooth's development and contributes and delivers the notes and documentation on the GitHub page. Unlike its peer, Fabric, Sawtooth is a nimble system that runs on small containers. For Hyperledger Fabric 1.3, I had chosen a ECS instance from Alibaba Cloud with Ubuntu 16.0.4 64 Bit, 2 VCPU, 4 GB RAM and 40 GB disk space. I let the two block chains co-exist on the ECS instance, besides opening the two blockchain systems to the external world.

CONSOLE: Set up the Elastic Cloud Instance (some call it EC or ECS or EC2). In our case we have chosen a 64-bit Ubuntu 16.0.4 running on 2 VCPUs, 4 GB, 40 GB. You can select a downgraded version such as 1 VCPU, 2 GB RAM and 20 GB instance.

CONSOLE: Set a security group. Assign or create a new set of keys for the instance and download the keys. Ensure the keys are secure and only readable by you before using them

LOCAL: Secure the downloaded keys.

```
$ chmod 400 alikeys.pem
```

LOCAL: SSH (Secure Shell) into your new server instance.

```
$ ssh -i ~/nodejs/alikeys.pem root@xx.xx.xxx.xxx
```
You should see a similar greeting:
Welcome to Ubuntu 16.04.5 LTS (GNU/Linux 4.4.0-117-generic x86_64)
 * Documentation: https://help.ubuntu.com
 * Management: https://landscape.canonical.com
 * Support: https://ubuntu.com/advantage
Welcome to Alibaba Cloud Elastic Compute Service !

 If is not a generic Ubuntu 16.0.4 64-Bit system, you may have chosen an incorrect instance. It will be a challenge in installing Sawtooth on such an instance.

INSTANCE: Create an user for other installations such as Hyperledger Sawtooth.

```
$ adduser devb
$ usermod -aG sudo devb
$ su - devb
```

INSTANCE: Install Apache2 on this new server

```
# -- This will ensure your instance is up to date
$ sudo apt update
# -- Install Apache webserver now
$ sudo apt-get install apache2
# -- Ensure SSL, headers, proxying ready for Apache
$ a2enmod ssl
$ a2enmod headers
$ a2enmod proxy_http
```

INSTANCE: Upon successful installation of Apache, the install kit sets up a 'htdocs' folder where the htmls get stored.

```
# -- /var/www
```

LOCAL: After Apache's installation, turn your attention to your local machine, fire up a web browser and check out the instance. The xx.xx.xxx.xxx represents the IPv4 address you can get from the console.

```
http://xx.xx.xxx.xxx
```

INSTANCE:

```
# -- change the attributes of the web root folder
$ sudo chmod -R 755 /var/www
$ cd /var/www
$ sudo chown root:devb *
```

INSTANCE: If you are planning on pointing your domain name to this instance, this is the right time change the apache configuration file.

```
$ cd /etc/apache2/sites-available
$ nano 000-default.conf
$ systemctl restart apache2
```

INSTANCE: Sawtooth expects a few prerequisites installed before attempting to install and finetune itself. As you may have noticed, the ECS instance chosen is a relatively small resource intensive instance and I intend to show you what it entails to run Sawtooth with no other frills - a barebones Ubuntu 16.0.4 instance equipped with Apache running barebones Hyperledger Sawtooth.

```
# -- if you have an earlier installation
# -- or even a failed installation
$ sudo rm /var/lib/dpkg/lock
# -- on with the Sawtooth installation
$ sudo apt-key adv --keyserver
hkp://keyserver.ubuntu.com:80 --recv-keys
8AA7AF1F1091A5FD
```

```
$ sudo add-apt-repository 'deb
http://repo.sawtooth.me/ubuntu/1.0/stable xenial
universe'

# -- ensure your instance is up to date with the
# -- suggested repository
$ sudo apt update
$ sudo apt-get install -y sawtooth
# -- clean up
$ sudo apt autoremove
```

INSTANCE: It's a good idea to take an inventory of what all you installed with Sawtooth.

```
$ sudo apt search sawtooth
```

 For Sawtooth to perform Blockchain operations, it needs Transaction Processors, Consensus mechanism, Sawtooth CLI, REST API, SDK, Validator and some examples.

```
Sorting... Done
Full Text Search... Done
...
python3-sawtooth-block-info/xenial 1.0.5-1 all
  Sawtooth Block Info Transaction Processor
python3-sawtooth-cli/xenial,now 1.0.5-1 all [installed,automatic]
  Sawtooth CLI
python3-sawtooth-ias-client/xenial 1.0.5-1 all
  Sawtooth Intel Attestation Service Client
python3-sawtooth-ias-proxy/xenial 1.0.5-1 all
  Sawtooth Intel Attestation Service Proxy
python3-sawtooth-identity/xenial 1.0.5-1 all
  Sawtooth Identity Transaction Processor
python3-sawtooth-intkey/xenial,now 1.0.5-1 all [installed,automatic]
  Sawtooth Intkey Python Example
python3-sawtooth-manage/xenial 0.8.8-1 all
  Sawtooth Lake Management Library
python3-sawtooth-poet-cli/xenial,now 1.0.5-1 all [installed,automatic]
  Sawtooth PoET CLI
```

```
python3-sawtooth-poet-common/xenial,now 1.0.5-1 all [installed,automatic]
  Sawtooth PoET Common Modules
python3-sawtooth-poet-core/xenial,now 1.0.5-1 all [installed,automatic]
  Sawtooth Core Consensus Module
python3-sawtooth-poet-families/xenial,now 1.0.5-1 all [installed,automatic]
  Sawtooth Transaction Processor Families
python3-sawtooth-poet-sgx/xenial 1.0.5-1 amd64
  Sawtooth PoET SGX Enclave
python3-sawtooth-poet-simulator/xenial,now 1.0.5-1 all [installed,automatic]
  Sawtooth PoET Simulator Enclave
python3-sawtooth-rest-api/xenial,now 1.0.5-1 all [installed,automatic]
  Sawtooth REST API
python3-sawtooth-sdk/xenial,now 1.0.5-1 all [installed,automatic]
  Sawtooth Python SDK
python3-sawtooth-settings/xenial,now 1.0.5-1 all [installed,automatic]
  Sawtooth Settings Transaction Processor
python3-sawtooth-signing/xenial,now 1.0.5-1 all [installed,automatic]
  Sawtooth Signing Library
python3-sawtooth-validator/xenial,now 1.0.5-1 all [installed,automatic]
  Sawtooth Validator
python3-sawtooth-xo/xenial,now 1.0.5-1 all [installed,automatic]
  Sawtooth XO Example
sawtooth/xenial,now 1.0.5 all [installed]
  Hyperledger Sawtooth Distributed Ledger
sawtooth-intkey-tp-go/xenial 1.0.5 all
  Sawtooth Intkey TP Go
sawtooth-noop-tp-go/xenial 1.0.5 all
  Sawtooth Noop TP Go
sawtooth-sabre/xenial 0.1.2 amd64
  Sawtooth Sabre Transaction Processor
sawtooth-smallbank-tp-go/xenial 1.0.5 all
  Sawtooth Smallbank TP Go
sawtooth-xo-tp-go/xenial 1.0.5 all
  Sawtooth Go XO TP
...
```

INSTANCE: You will find similar steps in the Sawtooth Documentation. I may have repeated some of the setup steps in this chapter. The next steps generate the public and private keys for the Validator.

The Validator recognizes those "Transactors" who present their transactions authenticated by the public key. Transactors can be machines or people that offer the transactions.

```
$ sawtooth keygen
# -- response
# -- creating key directory: /home/devb/.sawtooth/keys
# -- private key
# -- writing file: /home/devb/.sawtooth/keys/devb.priv
# -- public certificate
# -- writing file: /home/devb/.sawtooth/keys/devb.pub
```

INSTANCE: Generate the genesis batch file for the Validator.

```
$ sudo sawset genesis --key
~/.sawtooth/keys/devb.priv
# -- response
# -- Generated config-genesis.batch
```

INSTANCE: Generate the keys for the Validator.

```
$ sudo sawadm keygen
# -- response
# -- writing file: /etc/sawtooth/keys/validator.priv
# -- writing file: /etc/sawtooth/keys/validator.pub
```

INSTANCE: Configuring Sawtooth
If the config directory has a file named "validator.toml", then the validator uses the settings when it starts.

- By default, the config directory is /etc/sawtooth/
- Sawtooth installation adds a few examples in that folder

- View the folder and rename or copy the files as extension TOML.
- TOML files are the same as YAML files. TOML convention used is like YAML files. Edit the TOML files as necessary.

```
$ cd /etc/sawtooth
$ sudo cp cli.toml.example cli.toml
$ sudo cp path.toml.example path.toml
$ sudo cp rest_api.toml.example rest_api.toml
$ sudo cp log_config.toml.example log_config.toml
$ sudo cp settings.toml.example settings.toml
$ sudo cp validator.toml.example validator.toml
$ sudo cp xo.toml.example xo.toml
```

INSTANCE: Stop the services that may have auto started after the installation. Sawtooth generates many "systemd" files as part of the installation.

```
$ sudo systemctl stop sawtooth-validator.service
$ sudo systemctl stop sawtooth-rest-api.service
$ sudo systemctl stop sawtooth-settings-tp.service
$ sudo systemctl stop sawtooth-poet-validator-
registry-tp.service
```

INSTANCE: As part of cleanup, sometimes it is safer to the reboot the instance

```
$ exit
$ reboot
```

LOCAL: Back to the local machine where you will need to Secure Shell back into the instance.

```
$ ssh -i ~/nodejs/alikeys.pem root@xx.xx.xxx.xxx
```

INSTANCE:

```
$ su - devb
# - change the owner of this folder to the user
$ cd /etc/sawtooth
```

```
$ sudo chown devb:devb ./
$ sudo chown devb:devb *
$ sudo chown devb:devb .
```

INSTANCE: Start the Sawtooth Validator and RESTful services.

```
$ sudo sawtooth-validator -v --endpoint
localhost:8800
$ sawtooth-rest-api -v
```

INSTANCE: Test the service if it is up and running.

```
$ curl http://localhost:8008/blocks
```

INSTANCE: Check if Validator is using ports 8800 for other peers and 4004 for the transaction processor. You will also find the RESTful service listening on port 8008.

```
$ netstat -a
# -- Response
Active Internet connections (servers and established)
Proto Recv-Q Send-Q Local Address          Foreign Address        State
tcp      0      0 *:ssh                     *:*                    LISTEN
tcp      0      0 localhost:8800            *:*                    LISTEN
tcp      0      0 localhost:4004            *:*                    LISTEN
tcp      0      0 localhost:8008            *:*                    LISTEN
```

INSTANCE: Continuing with our Apache installation, I suggest using the "LetsEncrypt" service to secure the web application.

Install LetsEncrypt certificates.

```
# --- install lets encrypt
$ sudo apt-get update
$ sudo apt-get autoclean
# --- ./certbot-auto
$ sudo apt-get install letsencrypt
```

```
$ sudo add-apt-repository ppa:certbot/certbot
$ sudo apt-get update
$ sudo apt-get install certbot
```

```
# --- Now fetch the certificates
$ sudo certbot certonly --webroot -w /var/www/html -d
www.sawtoothsite.com
# --- certificates stored at
# -- /etc/letsencrypt/live/www.sawtoothsite.com/fullchain.pem
# -- /etc/letsencrypt/live/www.sawtoothsite.com/privkey.pem
```

Edit the apache configuration file.

```
$ sudo nano /etc/apache2/sites-enabled/
              000-default.conf
```

<VirtualHost *:80>
    ServerName www.sawtoothsite.com
    ServerAlias sawtoothsite.com www.sawtoothsite.com
    ServerAdmin devb@sawtoothsite.com
    DocumentRoot /var/www/html
</VirtualHost>

ServerName localhost

<IfModule mod_ssl.c>
<VirtualHost *:443>
    ServerName sawtoothsite.com
    ServerAlias sawtoothsite.com *.sawtoothsite.com
    ServerAdmin sawtooth@sawtooth
    DocumentRoot /var/www/html

    RequestHeader set X-Forwarded-Proto "https"

    Include /etc/letsencrypt/options-ssl-apache.conf
    SSLCertificateFile
    /etc/letsencrypt/live/www.sawtoothsite.com/fullchain.pem
    SSLCertificateKeyFile
        /etc/letsencrypt/live/www.sawtoothsite.com/privkey.pem

```
</VirtualHost>
</IfModule>

ProxyPass /sawtooth http://localhost:8008
ProxyPassReverse /sawtooth http://localhost:8008
RequestHeader set X-Forwarded-Path "/sawtooth"
```

 Now set the Apache with the new certificates and restart Apache.

```
$ sudo certbot --apache -d sawtoothsite.com
-d www.sawtoothsite.com
$ sudo apachectl restart
```

LOCAL: Check the URL on your local web browser to see if Sawtooth is accessible through https://www.sawtoothsite.com/sawtooth/blocks

Troubleshooting

If the validator and REST-API do not show up, it may be necessary to bring down the services, regenerate the keys and rerun the services.

```
$ sudo systemctl stop sawtooth-settings-tp
$ sudo systemctl enable sawtooth-settings-tp
$ sudo systemctl stop sawtooth-poet-validator-
registry-tp
$ sudo systemctl enable sawtooth-poet-validator-
registry-tp
$ sudo systemctl stop sawtooth-validator
$ sudo systemctl enable sawtooth-validator
$ sudo systemctl stop sawtooth-rest-api.service
$ sudo systemctl enable sawtooth-rest-api.service
```

```
$ sudo sawadm keygen --force
$ sudo sawadm genesis
$ sudo sawtooth-validator -v --endpoint
localhost:8800
$ sawtooth-rest-api -v
```

Besides installing Hyperledger Sawtooth, this chapter also walks you through the steps needed to setup Apache and TLS / SSL certificates so you can access the site safely. The makers of Sawtooth intended it to run behind Apache and not not expose its services directly to the external world. Through the reverse proxy you can direct all communications to the Sawtooth REST service.

***

WHAT'S WITH THE BIRDS?

As you can imagine, the last one year was far from easy, the constant churn in my head and at GitHub ensured that. Between us and the birds is the blinding truth that when our minds soar to different heights, their wings lift them there. The flight of the mind has its own story. The flight of birds has intrigued man since the beginning of days. In observing their nature, the ancients often ranked these small wonders to the great divine. Hamsa, the swan, at one time represented the absolute. Zeus, as swan, met Leda, and born was their child - Helen of Troy. Unlike the eagle, the lapwing, known for its slow, irregular wing beat in flight, makes a shrill, wailing cry, "Did you do it?" "Did you do it right?"

***

REFERENCE

Copyrights and Trademarks acknowledged:

REST - REpresentational State Transfer is an architectural style that defines a set of constraints and properties based on HTTP. LetsEncrypt is a registered TM of the Linux Foundation.

Cover and Back cover images:
Portions copyright Graphic Resources S.L.

Reference:
Wealth Management: The Financial Advisor's Guide to Investing and Managing Your Client's Assets / Edition 1 by Harold R. Evensky, International Association for Financial. ISBN-10: 0786304782, ISBN-13: 9780786304783.

Download(s):
All downloads are from GitHub repositories.

https://github.com/devbnj/Permissioned-Blockchain
https://github.com/devbnj/fabric-cloud/
https://github.com/devbnj/sawtooth-cloud/

INDEX

ABOUT THE AUTHOR

Dev, like many other authors, was indoctrinated into the art of writing. Dev has written for several journals, periodicals and books in the past. Dev lives with his wife and children in the northeast United States and is a prolific reader.

www.ingramcontent.com/pod-product-compliance
Lightning Source LLC
Chambersburg PA
CBHW051049050326
40690CB00006B/662